CONCILIUM

VATICAN II: A FORGOTTEN FUTURE?

Edited by
Alberto Melloni and Christoph Theobald

SCM Press · London

Published by SCM Press, 9–17 St Albans Place, London N1 0NX

Copyright © Stichting Concilium

English translations copyright © 2005 SCM-Canterbury Press Ltd

All rights reserved. No part of this publication may be
reproduced, stored in a retrieval system, or transmitted,
in any form or by any means, electronic, mechanical, photocopying,
recording or otherwise, without the prior written permission of
Stichting Concilium, Erasmusplein 1,
6525 HT Nijmegen, The Netherlands

ISBN 0 334 03085 4

Printed and bound in Great Britain by William Clowes Ltd, Beccles, Suffolk

Concilium Published February, April, June, October
December

Contents

Introduction
    ALBERTO MELLONI AND CHRISTOPH THEOBALD   7

I. Vatican II Forty Years On: Waning Relevance?   9

Vatican II and its History
    GIUSEPPE ALBERIGO   9

Vatican II and Theology
    ANDRÉS TORRES QUEIRUGA   21

II. Vatican II Today?: What is its Core?   35

'The Others': Ecumenism and Religions
    MAURO VELATI   35

Gaudium et Spes: the Forgotten Future of a Revolutionary Document
    ERIC BORGMAN   48

Forty Years Later: What has become of the Ecclesiological Reforms envisaged by Vatican II?
    HERVÉ LEGRAND   57

The Signs of the Times
    JOSÉ COMBLIN   73

III. The Future of Vatican II   87

The Theological Options of Vatican II: Seeking an 'Internal'
Principle of Interpretation
   CHRISTOPH THEOBALD   87

Is the Second Vatican Council Forgotten?
   HANS KÜNG   108

The Ignored 'Text'
On the Hermeneutics of the Second Vatican Council
   PETER HÜNERMANN   118

IV. A Panel on Vatican II Tomorrow   137

Vatican II Today
   JOSEPH DORÉ   137

Humanity – Centre and Summit of the Earth
   LUKAS VISCHER   148

Contributors   153

Introduction

ALBERTO MELLONI AND CHRISTOPH THEOBALD

Could things have been different? Perhaps not: they have certainly not been different in the aftermath of the great councils, and so in the aftermath of a council as great as Vatican II the jury remains out, still debating within and between generations. Councils – and so 'the Council' – are the touchstone: for the experience of faith, for theological reflection, for pastoral ministry, including the Petrine ministry. After Vatican II it is impossible to be – nor would anyone want to be – what we are without taking a clear stand on what the late Pope John Paul II called 'the grace event of the twentieth century' and which in his testament appears as the horizon opened on to the future of a new generation, one that neither celebrates nor remembers the Council but can still only discern its own sensibilities in the light of a hope that is wholly and solely post-conciliar.

For this generation too, so the late Pope's testamentary notes said, the Council will offer a future – even if it is a future that seems to be quickly forgotten: as early as 1965 the young theologian Joseph Ratzinger, a new member of the Board of *Concilium*, to be elected to the papal throne precisely forty years after the birth of this conciliar endeavour, was stigmatizing simplifications of Vatican II, which almost made it out to be the threshold of a new 'You have heard it said . . . but I say to you . . .'; then less than ten years later Paul VI reacted by breaking communion with the noisy Lefebvre minority, rather than accepting any relativization of the obedience due to Vatican II. Today the tendencies, tensions, and vital concerns that move the planetary body of the Church are not these: the tumultuous phase of the Council's reception no longer recognizes the polemical issues of the first two post-conciliar decades; and the phobic obsession that seeks at all costs to 'fix' Vatican II in an absolute and unchangeable continuity (historical irony: this was just the objection the Protestants made to Trent) resurfaces wherever the indecipherable logical processes of ecclesiastical power try to find the *casus belli* for an improbable season of historical-theological revisionism.

Nevertheless, the new generation – the one that comes after John Paul II, the last Bishop of Rome to have been a Council Father – runs the risk of seeing the future that belongs to it go up in smoke: the many voices pointing to Vatican II and the fortieth anniversary of its closure as the subject-matter for Benedict XVI's first encyclical seem to support this concern, to which this volume of *Concilium* offers its own choral and polyphonic response.

It has seemed necessary to us to venture into the tangle of the historicization of Vatican II: the work of elaborating a 'History of the Council', to which Cardinal Tucci in *La Civiltà Cattolica* and Fr Vallin in *Recherches de sciences religieuses* have devoted impassioned critical comments, has in fact opened up a route that remains essential if the hermeneutic of the Council is not to be allowed to slip into a virtual whirl of fragments, out-of-context quotations, glosses, and case-histories, at the end of which the Council can be accused of anything – including the 'fact' that, by 'only' deploring and not condemning anti-Semitism, it sanctioned its legitimization, to the advantage of those who, lurking in whatever corner of the ecclesial framework, love to flirt with minimizing the Council for the sake of their own rehabilitation.

In second place, it appeared essential to solicit reflection on the ways in which the balances of Christian experience intuited by Vatican II have been re-assessed: this is a reflection that in recent years has seen the emergence of many contributions as the anniversaries of the Council's Constitutions and Decrees have called for annotations and analyses – and which here, far from any pretence at completeness, is addressed only in reference to certain sensitive, delicate, or ambiguous issues.

Finally, there is the problem of discussions on hermeneutics and on the basic theological options for Christian experience and the life of faith: because if the Council was truly an event, then it would really be unpardonable arrogance to suppose that what Catholics (and not only they) have seen in the light of that event does not constitute an essential element in situating Vatican II in its true place in the development of the life of the Church.

Two profound and different voices – one of a theologian bishop of the post-conciliar era and the other of a pastor who was an observer at Vatican II – close this volume, almost as an invitation to each one of us to formulate and find our own position in relation to the event that as such is history and therefore living tissue of the way in which the Church becomes itself.

Translated by Paul Burns

I. Vatican II Forty Years On: Waning Relevance?

Vatican II and its History

GIUSEPPE ALBERIGO

I. The conciliar experience

In 1959 Pope John XXIII invited the Catholic episcopate to take on an active role at the level of the universal Church in the preparation of the future Council: it was the Pope himself who insisted on guaranteeing the effective freedom of this consultation. During the months the process lasted, however, the secrecy of Pius XII's style of government still prevailed, while the transition from this to an attitude of inquiry was having trouble in making headway.

The Pope wanted Vatican II to be the bishops' Council, but what did this mean? The distance between the view of a small number who proposed that such a re-evaluation had to be theologically based and that of those who were content with disciplinary adjustments, aimed at making each bishop a pope in his own diocese, was immense. Almost everyone resentfully denounced the rise of religious orders, demanded the suppression of the permanence of parish priests, a better distribution of clergy, and so on. This tendency, shared by the great majority, pointed to the completion of Vatican I, while the first sought, more or less explicitly, an effective collegiality.

Almost all the bishops came to the Council in some trepidation. Their reasons were various: they did not know the city of Rome; in the *aula*, the huge basilica of St Peter, they were seated next to unknown neighbours (in alphabetical order of surnames), as John Carmel Heenan, Bishop of Liverpool, observed in his notes.[1] Furthermore, they had difficulty understanding Latin – particularly that of 'foreigners' – and their understanding of the arguments under discussion was limited and, to be honest, out of date, so that they soon enough found the debates boringly repetitive – particularly those who were not very agile in distinguishing among various points of view. Finally, hardly anyone knew what the 'project' of the Council was, nor how long they would have to be far away from home, incurring considerable discomfort and expense. The numerous diaries kept bear witness, especially at the beginning, to a passive, 'student' attitude. They were taking part in a solemn and significant event, but they could not clearly discern its plan.

They found the General Congregations 'tiresome' occasions to attend, given that their main function was to listen: the overwhelming majority of bishops never spoke at all during the three hundred Congregations. Their diaries, here and there, note their daily fatigue, which brought on boredom and the occasional nap.... Some were even impatient and acerbic.[2] Several hundred bishops however were involved in the Commissions, where there was far more frequent occasion to be active. Then there were the meetings of Episcopal Conferences, at which – at least – they did not have the problem of understanding Latin or other badly understood or completely unknown languages.

With all this, Vatican II turned out to be the greatest achievement of the Catholic episcopate and the Holy Spirit. In the end there is no denying that only the conversion of the bishops, under the guidance of the Spirit, made possible the progress (or, perhaps one should say, the 'overturning') from the inert and timid passivity of the replies sent to Rome by so many hundreds of bishops in 1960 to the body of decisions approved by the Council. It is right and proper to recognize the limitations and even defects of the Council's conclusions, but it is impossible not to see with the naked eye the qualitative leap that occurred between the views with which the bishops replied to John XXIII's invitation, which indicated the problems the Council would have to tackle, and the image of Christianity and the Church that the Council put forward, precisely as a result of the consensus of virtually all of these same bishops. Slowly and almost imperceptibly, a general climate developed, in which a large number of bishops were predisposed to see Vatican II as a unique occasion for the renewal of the Church, along the lines indicated in the preceding decades by the liturgical, biblical, and ecumenical movements, by the question of human resources, and under the pressure of the secularization of society.

The excitement of the climate generated in Rome by the prolonged presence of over two thousand bishops, with an equal number of *periti* – theologians, canon lawyers, historians – and a huge number of journalists demonstrating the extent of public interest, in its turn played an ever-increasing role in informing the bishops and helping them to make up their minds. While in their official place of work, the *aula*, the great majority of bishops could only play a passive listening role, very soon, 'outside', numerous more interesting and accessible venues were found: conferences, study sessions, assemblies of Bishops' Conferences, exchanges at meals or on buses during the daily journey to and from St Peter's. These were all circumstances in which the bishops moved out from their limited – if not narrow – horizon of running a diocese, discovered the larger (perhaps unknown) problems of the universal Church, encountered spiritual and pastoral experiences other than their own, and could not fail to face up to a wide, uneven, and many-faceted world.

The four years of shuttle between diocese and Council (three months in Rome, nine at home) delivered the opportunity to compare the attitudes adopted in the Council on the burning issues (collegiality, episcopal consecration, responsibility for the universal Church, relations with the laity, war and peace) and the criteria followed within their local diocesan churches. The comparison was often embarrassing, requiring a readiness to self-criticism to which bishops were hardly accustomed. An unfamiliar experience that caught many bishops off guard was that of conflicts. Too many of them were used to a quiet and even flat vision of Christianity and the Church, regarding differences of opinion and conflictive ideas as a defect typical of lay society. In any case, they saw the Council as an ordered assembly, soon to be over, as indeed Roman Curial sources had encouraged them to do. According to their diaries, the actual experience of participating in Vatican II proved to be full of powerful implications and feelings: joy, concern, pride, apprehension.[3] Day by day, a conciliar understanding matured in the minds of the great majority. An understanding that the Council and the hopes it had awakened were in the hands of the bishops, that they – with the Pope – were really responsible for the proclamation of the gospel at that moment in history, that – in short – each one of them had a role to play in an extraordinary event, one they had never imagined.

II. Chronicles, documentation

Vatican II attracted an extraordinary degree of media attention.[4] Even during the progress of the assembly volumes that gathered together the main journalistic reports in various languages were published. These provided a first level of understanding of the Council's doings, giving a considerable impression of what went on in the Council behind the final published documents, detailing their multi-cultural composition and the various positions adopted.

The documentation produced by the Council was immense and is difficult to quantify; still less has it been possible to keep complete copies of it. Every day scores of texts originating both inside and outside the assembly were produced and distributed. The Council Secretariat carried out a valuable and valiant work of collection, but it was unable to reach beyond the documentation that passed through its offices. A fortunate, timely, and farsighted decision by Paul VI gave the Vatican II Archive autonomy from the secret Vatican Archives and the strict rules governing them. This has allowed the documentation collected by the General Secretariat to be classified and, finally, made available to students. This was the condition that allowed the admirably prompt publication (something virtually unique in conciliar history!) of three series of Council Acts, comprising over sixty volumes.[5] The 'informal' documentation had a less secure fate: not having had the luck to pass through the Secretariat, it was scattered, at least initially. In fact many of those who took part in the Council kept – wholly or partially – their own documents, but others were unable or unwilling to do so, especially those who came from other continents, who were limited by air travel. Only in the last decade of the twentieth century was it possible to raise the matter of collecting and conserving all the 'informal' conciliar documentation, comprising very varied material, much of it of great value and, in any case, useful for integrating what can be learned from the 'formal' documents in the official archive.[6]

III. Vatican II as history

Beginning in 1988, almost twenty-five years after the end of Vatican II, a world-wide multi-cultural and interdisciplinary team was formed, with the aim of preparing a history that would reconstruct, on the basis of original documentation, the course of Vatican II from its first announcement in January 1959 to the solemn closure on 8 December 1965. This has been an experience of joint research and deepened understanding of the riches, limitations, and contradictions of Vatican II, carried out with rigorous methodology with regard to how the Council actually progressed. It has been possible to reveal the story of a multi-cultural assembly, the like of which has never before been known in the long history of councils. The dialectical tensions between majorities and minorities, between Council and Pope, between Council and Curia, between assembly and commissions, between bishops and theologians, between Council and public opinion, have all emerged. Equally, the difficulties deriving from the fact that the Council was dealing partly with subjects already considered, such as liturgy, tradition, and ecclesiology and partly with new considerations, such as religious freedom, relations with other religions, the place of the Church in contemporary society, which had given rise to anxieties on account of their novelty, have all been reconstructed in their whole extent. The life of the Council has been pieced together, virtually day by day, in such a way as to reveal the complex riches of the dialectic of the assembly.

The *History of the Second Vatican Council*[7] aims to establish how the Council actually developed and to nourish understanding, moving beyond the awareness of the participants and the lifetime of the generation that witnessed the event, and despite the 'hermeneutical jealousies' of the protagonists, who have been induced to condition their interpretation of the actions of the Council. We have been determined to bring about an analytical and at the same time overall understanding, not divided into sectors or fragments, of this great gathering. Equally important has been the History's function of stimulating fresh attention to and conserving the great number and variety of sources relating to Vatican II.

To get the History going, we also, during several years of research, had to find an adequate amount of information on the preparatory work, which, while it was going on, was hidden under an impenetrable cloak of secrecy. Only by doing this has it been possible to perceive the full significance of the influence the years 1959–62 had on the actual Council as such, to an extent unknown at previous councils.[8] In the same way we have tried to bring about an understanding of the different phases of the work of the Council.[9] Even when the arguments and problems were, as usual, interwoven, we have tried to avoid a schematic representation of them, preferring to respect the various overlays that often left the actions of the Council Fathers confused and mixed up.[10] Time and again particular aspects of the confrontations between the Fathers and the laborious drafting of the final documents have been brought to light. In this respect the most difficult choice was that of how to reflect and respect the various opinions expressed. While it was virtually impossible – largely because of the lack of information – to distinguish and assign different approaches during the preparatory years, increasingly differentiated convictions were evidenced from the first days of the Assemblies. It has therefore been incumbent on us to make every effort to document these differences and to describe them with the utmost fidelity.

We decide to move away from a 'chronicle-ized' presentation of the work of the Council, while not trying to reconstruct it either on the basis of the 'grid' of the sixteen final documents, which seemed the obvious course in the 1980s. We followed the division into four working sessions following the preparatory years, respecting as far as possible the process that marked the day-to-day activity of the members of the Council: discussions in General Congregation, the work of the Commissions, meetings of informal groups, information sessions, individual meetings. Only gradually did we become aware of the snares inherent in the long 'inter-session' periods, during which the activity of the Council went on, either in Commissions or through contacts among bishops and exchanges among theologians. Initially we attached our account of these periods to that of the previous full session of the Council; only toward the end of our work did we come to appreciate that the activity that took place between sessions – even while being a continuation of the previous period – spilled over inevitably into the next session of council debates and so should be attached to the beginning of the new period rather than to the end of the preceding one.

IV. New understandings

Alongside the research, we realized that the availability of fresh documentation provided unexpected opportunities for understanding, to the point of leading to really and truly new information, previously unknown. This happened with regard to the pre-preparatory consultation period (1959–60): it emerged that the Curia and Cardinal Tardini had proposed sending the bishops a questionnaire asking for suggestions as to the topics that should be discussed at the Council. John XXIII however rejected the proposal, preferring a completely free and unconditioned consultation, which produced more than two thousand pre-preparatory views. Research has also established that the contents of the views were analyzed by the Roman Curia in accordance with the procedure laid down by the then current Code of Canon Law, resulting in the views themselves being given a 'canonistic' slant.

As for the preparatory work proper (1960–62), it has been possible to reconstruct the activity of the Commissions, which, apart from that on the Laity and the Secretariat for Christian Unity, paralleled the Congregations of the Roman Curia. These Commissions, with the exception of the Secretariat, were all dominated by Cardinal Tardini and the proposals put forward by the Congregations. This aspect of our research required a thorough trawl through the archives, since in the *Acta et Documenta* the acts of the individual Commissions were not published.[12] Only now is it possible to realize the full extent of the work carried out by the Secretariat for Christian Unity in deepening the approach to the Council's themes with a view to an *'aggiornamento'* carried through in a 'pastoral' spirit and with ecumenical sensitivity. The weakness of the Central Commission has also come to light, showing that it did not in fact guide the preparatory work but limited itself to evaluating – even when the Council was just about to open and almost always passively – the extremely numerous and verbose texts produced by the Commissions.

Knowledge of the activity of the Preparatory Commissions has allowed us to see that John XXIII, while scrupulously respecting the autonomous responsibility of the organs established for the preparatory work, set a parallel preparation in motion, committing himself to outlining the features of the Council through his various public utterances from 1960 to 1962. Two different images of the Council have thereby emerged. On the one hand, a rapid Council (lasting just a few weeks) for the quick approval of the seventy-two preparatory *schemae*; on the other, a 'self-responsible' council, a 'new Pentecost', which the bishops would have to build day after day in freedom and through searching.

On this basis, helped by the annual meetings of the contributors and the publication of numerous preparatory studies, the first volume of the History, covering the years 1959–62, finally provides tools for understanding the complex pre-history of the Council, till then completely unknown. It has thus become possible to evaluate the considerable influence this exercised on the labours and conclusions of the Council itself.[13] Nevertheless, the preparation made a somewhat limited contribution to the riches, the participatory spirit, and the dynamism of the conciliar event.[14]

As to the work of the Council as such, knowledge of the sources demonstrates that the doctrinal evolution of the Fathers (and of their theologians) cannot be represented by a steadily ascending line but has to be expressed by several broken lines. This is particularly clear with regard to *De Ecclesia* and *De apostolatu laicorum* and also with respect to church-society relationships as envisaged from sociological, theological, and other viewpoints. Knowledge of the debates has shown that the impact of the experience, but also of the weakness, of the 'movements' (liturgical, ecumenical, biblical, for the advancement of the laity) was considerable. It would not be unreasonable to regard the movements of the first half of the twentieth century as a genuine 'pre-council'. On the other hand, post-modernist crisis diffidence also had a 'holding back' effect on the outcomes of theological research. This is clear in regard to episcopal collegiality, conceived rather as a counterweight to papal power than as a dimension of communion among local churches; also in regard to ecumenism, seen as Catholic 'attitudes' to other churches rather than a project of unity. Furthermore, what is still remarkable is the evidence of a lack of a theology of peace, or of marriage, or of any of the analogous 'social' questions, to which the 'social teaching' of the church had not provided satisfactory replies.

Deeper analysis of the documentation also led to a greater understanding of the outcomes. The most significant fact is the degree to which *aggiornamento* and pastoral considerations affected the work of the Council. Both were taken seriously by the bishops and, as a result, deeply influenced the spirit of the Council; they had less influence on the composition of the approved texts. The gathering slowly came to perceive the alternatives of an attitude of acceptance of the preparatory *schemae* and a spirit of enquiry. The great majority of the Fathers shared the decision not to issue condemnations and anathemas, which John XXIII had announced in October 1962. But working out texts suitable for expressing *aggiornamento* in a pastoral style and spirit proved a great deal more difficult.

Also significant was the emergence of a quest for rich and complex statements, but also of a gap between the event of the Council as a collective happening and the final decisions made by the assembly.[16] We came to see that the event of the Council could not be reduced to the body, wide though it was, of its decisions: the collegiality of the Council had much greater depth and coherence than the expression of it in *Lumen Gentium*. The Constitutions and Decrees do not reflect all the shades of opinion that had been expressed over the course of the Council. This was a more packed and significant 'event' than the *corpus* of its decisions and has not been exhausted by their formulation and approbation. This gap also results from the enormous expectations aroused in the period before the Council opened, meaning that the 'Council event' produced results simply by being announced, when it was not yet in existence.

V. A hermeneutical turning

Investigating the history of Vatican II opens up the possibility of a 'hermeneutical turning'. We have been able to move beyond fragmentary or episodic knowledge of daily affairs in the assembly, not simply because overlapping analysis of the sources – beside the *Acta Synodalia*, a great quantity of complementary documents emanating from the Council, but also personal ones, such as diaries and letters from Rome – has enriched our understanding, but above all because the resulting unitary and synthetic vision of the entire life of the assembly prevents over-emphasis on individual episodes or particular passages in the documents torn out of context and deprived of their complexity.[17]

In this way, we are offered the possibility of 'transverse' researches, which bring to light the recurring and often determining presence of crucial factors in the spirit of the Council: liturgical and ecclesiological renewal, reaching beyond the limitations of the two corresponding Constitutions; ecumenical concern, deeper and more consistent than that expressed in the decree *Unitatis redintegratio*; the rediscovery of the Word of God, expressed in more than *Dei Verbum*; the fundamental need for religious freedom, which the Fathers gradually came to appreciate, above all as a dimension of their Christian charter. With the comprehensive and critically comprehensible information on the activity of the Council at our disposal, it is possible to follow the very phenomenon of the evolution of the great majority of the Fathers as it happened, thus overcoming the risk of reducing it – or the temptation to do so – to single episodes, however picturesque.[19] It has been possible to reveal the profound 'turning' reached with the vote on 19 November 1962 on the *schema* on 'the two sources of Revelation', which showed the Fathers' determination to base their treatment of such a delicate question, the relationship between Scripture and Tradition, on a 'pastoral' approach.

Compiling the history of the Council has brought to light the deep 'unity' of the work of the Council, with the decisions it approved little by little shown to be as authoritative as they were partial. This both renders researches into the subject of the particular factors that inspired Vatican II and formed the weft that held together and unified its decisions possible and ensures the richness of their outcome. These factors are arguments that recurred throughout the Council's work, or at least through a major part of it. We are dealing with an approach required by the very nature of Vatican II, a council of pastoral reflection, not one of polemic against errors, a council of updating with a view to the future rather than completing existing structures, a council – ultimately – that expressed guidelines for the life of Christianity, but which did not lay down peremptory norms.

In the light of its history, we can state that Vatican II never had 'conciliarist' temptations: the assembly was consistently devout in its dealings with both John XXIII and Paul VI. Even in 'extreme cases', when the Council's outlook differed from the Pope's, there was never any conflict between them. Critical understanding of the history of the Council shows that conciliarity has been the primary and original content of Vatican II and of its heritage, which is why this is the correct perspective on its reception under the guidance of the Spirit.

The *History of Vatican II* aims to make a contribution to nourishing the fruitfulness and definitiveness of the 'conciliar' dimension of Christianity from the highest 'ecumenical' level –interfaith, that is – to its 'normal' level of the local community on the ground. A contribution to a reception based on and developed as 'conciliarity' and therefore poly-centred and creative, instead of a centralized and therefore inevitably bureaucratic approach. Understanding the experience of Vatican II is not an attempt to wall the Council up in the past but an intent to nourish the unending need for creative and courageous obedience to the Spirit on the part of the churches.

Translated by Paul Burns

Notes

1. 'This was our first day in our alloted places. Hitherto we had sat where we wished and naturally most bishops sat with colleagues from the same hierarchy. Corresponding with our numbered seats the voting papers would bear a number. Mine was S149. Because we were in new places we each felt very isolated. There was no English archbishop anywhere near me. After a few days when we came to know each other I realised that immediately behind me sat the Archbihop of Karachi. He is a highly intelligent and rather young man. We were able to discuss many propositions. But on that morning we were all strangers to each other.' (private notes on the Vatican Council, ISR).
2. Archbishop Florit noted on 10 Nov. 1964: 'I had a little nap' (unpublished, ISR). 'I went for a walk around the interior of St Peter's, so as not to have to listen to the nonsense talked by those ultramontane bishops, who reduce the gospel to a fairy story, dogmas to definitive formulations not from Revelation but from theologians' studies, the Faith to mere feeling, who do not recognize the Church's magisterium, who have a dislike for their own priesthood, and who claim to speak in the name of Jesus Christ': thus Bishop L. C. Borromeo of Pesaro in his diary for 23 Nov. 1962 (Buonasorte), in the grip of feelings induced by the vote on the *schema* on the 'two sources'. For his part, B. C. Butler, abbot of Downside, noted on 22 Nov. 1962 that he had had an encounter with Browne, who threatened to denounce him to the Holy Office on account of his position on 'the annunciation' (unpublished diary, ISR).
3. Archbishop Montini in his letter to his diocese dated 2 December 1962 stressed how '[t]his spiritual experience will certainly remain indelible for those who have the good fortune to take part in the council: gentle most of the time, strong and powerful at other times, dramatic occasionally, and also thoughtful and painful at certain moments. . . .'
4. Cf. J. Grootaers, 'Informelle Strukturen der Information am Vatikanum II', in *Biotope der Hoffnung. Zu Christentum und Kirche heute*, ed. N. Klein, H. R. Schlette, and K. Weber, Olten 1988, pp. 268–81.
5. *Acta et documenta concilio oecumenico Vaticano II apparando, series I (antepraeparatoria)*, Vatican Polyglot Press 1960–61; *Acta et documenta concilio oecumenico Vaticano II apparando, series II (praeparatoria*, 1964–5; *Acta Synodalia sacrosancti concilii oecumenici Vaticani II*, 1970–80, all ed. V. Carbone.

6. The archive of Vatican II was in 2000 integrated into the Secret Vatican Archive, while still keeping the status established by Paul VI: cf. S. Pagano, 'Riflessioni sulle fonti archivistiche del concilio Vaticano II. In margine ad una pubblicazione recente', *Cristianesimo nella Storia* 23 (2002) pp. 775–812. The compilation of an inventory of the archive itself is well advanced.
7. The History is published in several languages: Italian (Il Mulino, Bologna), German (Grünewald, Mainz), English (Orbis, Maryknoll, NY), French (Cerf, Paris), Spanish (Sígueme, Salamanca), Portuguese (Vozes, Petrópolis), and Russian (St. Andrew, Moscow). The main theological and historical reviews have devoted ample space to it.
8. A. Indelicato, *Difendere la dottrina o annunciare l'Evangelo*, Genoa 1992; J. O. Beozzo, *Cristianismo e iglesias de América Latina en vísperas del Vaticano II*, Costa Rica 1992; *À la veille du Concile Vatican II. Vota et réactions en Europe et dans le Catholicisme oriental*, ed. M. Lamberigts and C. Soetens, Louvain 1992; *Verso il Concilio Vaticano II*, Bologna 1993; *Il Vaticano II tra attese e celebrazione*, Bologna 1995.
9. *Per la storicizzazione del Vaticano II*, ed. G. Alberigo and A. Melloni, Bologna 1992; *Vatican II commence... Approches francophones*, ed. É. Fouilloux, Louvain 1993; *Der Beitrag der deutschsprachigen und osteuropäischen Länder zum zweiten vatikanischen Konzil*, ed. K. Wittstadt and W. Verschooten, Louvain 1996; *Les Commissions conciliaires à Vatican II*, ed. M. Lamberigts, C. Soetens and J. Grootaers, Louvain 1996; *Vatican II in Moscow (1959–1965)*, ed. A. Melloni, Louvain 1997, also pub. in Russian in Moscow; *Experience, Organisation and Bodies at Vatican II*, ed. M. T. Fattori and A. Melloni, Louvain 2000; *Herausforderung-Aggiornamento zur Rezeption des Zweiten Vatikanischen Konzils*, ed. A. Autiero, Altenberge 2000; *Volti di fine concilio. Studi di storia e teologia sulla conclusione del Vaticano II*, ed. J. Doré and A. Melloni, Bologna 2000.
10. M. Velati, *Una difficile transizione. Il cattolicesimo tra unionismo ed ecumenismo (1952–1964)*, Bologna 1996; M. Paiano, *Liturgia e società nel Novecento. Percorsi del movimento liturgico di fronte ai processi di secolarizzazione*, Rome 2000; R. Burigana, *La Bibbia nel Concilio. La redazione della costituzione 'Dei Verbum' del Vaticano II*, Bologna 1998; G. Turbanti, *Un Concilio per il mondo moderno. La redazione della costituzione pastorale 'Gaudium et spes' del Vaticano II*, Bologna 2000; A. Melloni, *L'altra Roma. Politica e S. Sede durante il concilio Vaticano II (1959–1965)*, Bologna 2000; N. Buonasorte, 'Per la "pura, piena, integra fede cattolica": il p. V. A. Berto al concilio Vaticano II', *Cristianesimo nella Storia* 22 (2001) pp. 111–151; S. Scatena, *La fatica della libertà. L'elaborazione della dichiarazione «Dignitatis humanae» sulla libertà religiosa del Vaticano II*, Bologna 2003; M. Faggioli, *Il vescovo e il concilio. Modello episcopale e aggiornamento nella storia del decreto 'Christus Dominus' del Vaticano II*, Bologna 2005.
11. *Storia del concilio Vaticano II – I. Il cattolicesimo verso una nuova stagione. L'annuncio e la preparazione (gennaio 1959–settembre 1962)*, Bologna 1995, pp. 17–176.

12. *Ibid.*, pp. 177–526.
13. *Storia del concilio Vaticano II – II. La formazione della coscienza conciliare (ottobre 1962–settembre 1963)*, Bologna 1996. A test of such conditionings was provided by the dropping of the 'Döpfner plan' (1963–4), which – by relaunching the reduction in the number of *schemae* worked out in 1962 – would have sought to concentrate (and shorten) the work on the main subjects.
14. So it became clear that the preparatory work had caused reactions principally in confrontation with Roman and Curial hegemony producing a revindication of the responsibility of the episcopate. Suffice to evoke the sending-back of the elections to the Commissions (13 Oct. 1962) and the discovery of episcopal conferences by the majority of the bishops.
15. *Storia del concilio Vaticano II – III. Il concilio adulto (settembre 1963–settembre 1964)*, Bologna 1998. Knowledge of the work of the Commissions is still incomplete, however: see G. Turbanti, 'Quellenbericht über die Konzilskommissionen', in *Der Beitrag der deutschsprachigen...*, pp.251–8.
16. *Storia del concilio Vaticano II – IV. La chiesa come comunione (settembre 1964 – settembre 1965)* and *V. Concilio di transizione (settembre-dicembre 1965)*, Bologna 1999 and 2001.
17. On this point the discussion on the meaning of *subsistit in* in LG 8 is typical, conducted as it was without reference to the context of the whole of the work of the Council, as A. von Teuffenbach does in *Die Bedeutung des 'subsistit in'(LG 8). Zum Selbstverständnis der katholischen Kirche*, Munich 2002, justly criticized by L. Sartori, 'Osservazioni sull'ermeneutica del 'subsistit in' proposta da Alexandra von Teuffenbach', *Rassegna di Teologia* 45 (2004) pp.279–81. So too the fact and significance of the steering vote on 30 Oct. 1963, of the 'black week' in October 1964, or of the tensions in 1965 over religious freedom and over peace should now be placed in the context of and re-examined in the framework of the entire Council.
18. For this purpose instruments such as *Constitutionis dogmaticae* Lumen Gentium *Synopsis historica*, ed. G. Alberigo and F. Magistretti, Bologna 1975, are essential, as are the *Indices verborum et locutionum Decretorum Concilii Vaticani II*, Istituto per le Scienze Religiose, 11 vols, Bologna 1968–80; P. Delhaye, M. Gueret, P. Tombeur, *Concilium Vaticanum II. Concordance, Index, Listes de fréquence, Tables comparatives*, Louvain 1974.
19. Of which the Frings–Ottaviani polemic on the subject of the Holy Office (8 Nov. 1963) is typical.

Vatican II and Theology

ANDRÉS TORRES QUEIRUGA

Theology *of* the Council, theology *in* the Council, theology *after* the Council: all these are possible approaches. The first has undoubtedly been the most prevalent – as history of the whole event and of each of its documents; as 'achievements', deficiencies, or 'balances' struck between different tendencies; as what has been achieved and what is still to do. All this is necessary work and has borne much fruit. As the title of this volume indicates, however, the time – almost half a century – that has elapsed calls for it to be completed, by setting it in a wide historical perspective that will allow its epoch-making significance to be appreciated. Hence the open and accessible title of this contribution.

I. Act and text

This title actually tries to place the Council in the broad sweep that, since the advent of 'modernity', has 'shaken the foundations' (Tillich) of culture and religion. More than an assemblage of specific teachings, the Council was an event that affected the entire being of the believing community and also had intense repercussions on universal culture. The great act of the Council itself goes far beyond the letter of its texts, which reveal the real meaning behind them only within that act and its breadth of intention. Hans Küng appreciated this when he placed Vatican II as a decisive juncture in the paradigm shift brought about by the Reformation and Modernity.[1] And Giuseppe Alberigo has on various occasions stressed the 'qualitative priority of the conciliar event even in relation to its own decisions.'[2]

Running through history in seven-league boots of course always involves the risk of making simplistic generalizations. But my sole purpose here is to point out the main lines leading from the break-up of the medieval synthesis to determine the situation of the Council and mark out its intention. That, basically, is what it was about. The great medieval synthesis, inheritor of the pre-modern past, began to unravel with the coming of a new historical era. The inrush of Modernity (which Karl Jaspers classifies as the last great historical break, on a par with hominization, the dawn of the Neolithic, or the 'axis time'),[3] had faced Christianity with the choice between making a radical change or remaining paralyzed in a dead past. The task was so huge that the Churches were highly resistant to and always late in tackling it.

The Reformation, through and alongside Humanism, provided the first major shock: we had to go back to scripture, the thrust of which was threatened with burial under the solid mass of the institution and the weight of tradition. This was its great contribution, but it proved insufficient, since, while it brought about the sunset of the medieval system, it discerned the dawning of modern changes only from afar. Experience of the Bible and the new Humanist sensitivity shattered traditional formalisms, but their concepts did not break the moulds of the old world-view. Much later, Bultmann was to sum up the emotion and disquiet that biblical criticism had made increasingly obvious, in the powerful symbolical expression 'demythologization'. Neither its monotony, denounced by Jaspers, nor its privatizing tendency, criticized by political theology, should obscure the real power of a summons that takes us well beyond Bultmann's own 'system'. The essence of his proposal is beyond debate to the degree that it requires a radical revision of the whole Christian world-view, since it is still true that 'we cannot use electric light and wireless sets or employ modern clinical and medicinal methods in treating illnesses, while at the same time believing in the New Testament world of spirits and miracles'.[4]

Modernity effectively imposed a further step, the need for which became apparent with the new science, the new historical criticism, the new sociology, and the new philosophy. The enormous pressure this cultural shift exerted undoubtedly and decisively determined the evolution of theology, filled as it was with discoveries and refusals, advances and retreats, 'always a bit behind the times', 'always a bit outdated and antiquated (*altmodisch*)'.[5] Orthodoxy, pietism, enlightenment, liberalism, neo-orthodoxy, secularization and the like in the Protestant camp; baroque scholasticism, neo-Thomism, Modernism, biblical, patristic, and liturgical movements, *nouvelle théologie* and so forth in the Catholic: all showed the ups and downs of an ever-sought and never-quite-achieved meeting of minds, always renewed and not infrequently suppressed.

The greatness of Vatican II lay in the fact that, for the first time and in an official manner, it recognized the situation by proclaiming the need for an *aggiornamento* and thereby legitimating intentions to bring it about. This is its indelible *act*.

II. The challenge of the act: God and the autonomy of creation

This is also its most decisive significance. And here we have to search for it, which implies a hermeneutical challenge with, in my view, two main aspects: to calibrate the global impact of the Council event and to seek the living and radiant nucleus of its proposal.

The first calls for an accurate dialectic to distinguish between its overall impulse and its specific solutions. The latter could not in a few years perform what should have been a centuries-long task. The Council, rather than a complete response, was the hole in the dyke that had held back the turbulent waters of a renovation always waiting around the corner. It was not possible to put everything in its proper place, and a certain sensation of bewilderment and incompleteness was inevitable. It is not surprising that the assessment made by *Concilium* itself five years after the Council recognized that '[t]he walls of the ecclesiastical Jericho have not come tumbling down despite the theological trumpets'.[6] Cardinal Suenens himself observed that 'We have become more sensitive to all that Vatican II laid down but did not fully resolve'.[7] Many went much further, in a reaction of fear and puzzlement, preferring the old certainties of 'the fleshpots of Egypt' to the adventure of a new exodus. And, unfortunately, this reaction gained the upper hand in recent church policy.

This was not the choice *Concilium* made. A minimum of historical understanding shows that, despite everything, going back is not an option. And there is no way of not recognizing the enormous advance represented by the impact of the Council. We may be dissatisfied with what remains undone, but we must still be fair to what was achieved, which is a great deal. There is new climate: a believer from the 1950s dropped into today's world would in many ways have the impression of being in a different Church. There is a new inner freedom: let's be frank, despite all the institutional barriers – how many priests feel the slightest scruple in not following the directives in the latest document on the Eucharist to the letter? Or what theologians would not now draw a distinction between the juridical inconveniencies and the legitimacy of their inner conscience faced with a Roman condemnation of their writings? There is a new theological creativity: compare, for example, a present-day Christology with any of the pre-conciliar manuals.

This is where the second aspect ties in: trying by some means to define the central intuition that tells us what the deep-down intention of the Council was. This is not easy to determine, but, as we progress in doing so, it becomes more practicable to open up the right paths along which the Council took the first steps. In this sense, I have the impression that a passage from *Gaudium et spes*, its section 36, can provide an approach to what we are looking for, in that it points straight to what, in my opinion, forms the decisive thrust of Modernity: the *autonomy* of the world. I quote (abbreviated) to show its positive evaluation and its warning:

> If by autonomy of earthly affairs we mean that created things and societies themselves enjoy their own laws and values which must be gradually deciphered, put to use, and regulated by human beings, then it is entirely right to demand that autonomy. Such is not merely required by modern man, but harmonizes also with the will of the Creator. For by the very circumstances of their having been created, all things are endowed with their own stability, truth, goodness, proper laws, and order. Man must respect these as he isolates them by the appropriate methods of the individual sciences or arts. . . .

But if the expression, the independence of temporal affairs, is taken to mean that created things do not depend on God, and that man can use them without any reference to their Creator, anyone who acknowledges God will see how false such an interpretation is. For without the Creator, the creature would disappear. For their part however all believers of whatever religion have always heard His revealing voice in the discourse of creatures. But when God is forgotten the creature itself grows unintelligible.

A few observations. The quote comes from a Constitution that was not even envisaged by the Preparatory Commission but which emerged from the inner dynamic of the Council, imposed by the new historical situation.[8] It supposes a clear and decisive acceptance that this autonomy is 'entirely right'. This extends to all orders of existence: 'created things and societies themselves'. It finally forms a necessary hermeneutical criterion: 'the appropriate methods of the individual sciences or arts'.

There is nonetheless an important clarification to be made. The Council is inviting acceptance of a reality – autonomy – that supposes an irreversible advance of the human spirit; it underpins modern transformation but does not of itself justify all its consequences. It calls for acceptance of autonomy insofar as it represents *common discovery and undoubted advance*; it uses it as a basis for working out a contemporary theology, in critical dialogue with the various solutions put forward in Modernity (at this level, 'post-modernity' functions as an avatar within Modernity, not as its successor).[9] In other words, there is scope for being very critical of many of the proposals of modern culture (just as it is with those of the Churches); solutions, though, can never turn things back: they have to be built forward, starting from modern culture.[10] A fatal trap into which theological discussion has too often fallen is taking 'Modernity' as a homogenous whole and, seizing on its defects, exaggerations, and even perversions, discrediting the whole endeavour of modernization as such. This causes questions that affect the basic relationship of revelation to culture to be pushed aside, changing them into mere domestic disputes or outdated confessional controversies.

Ultimately, this is what the Council was saying. It set no limits to the legitimacy of the autonomy 'required by modern man'; what it did do, from the religious point of view, is demand its proper dialectical integration with the Creator's plan. But stating this is much easier than bringing it about. Historically, the first solution was *deism*: the novelty of autonomy was felt with such force that God was relegated to a distant and abstract heaven, something that true religious understanding could not accept. But by then the alternative could not be a return to the traditional 'god', who now proved incompatible with the *legitimate* autonomy of the world. The real challenge consisted – and still consists[11] – in showing that this incompatibility stemmed from the false image of a 'mythic' and interventionist god. What was needed was to show that the famous *etsi Deus non daretur* in reality meant only, *etsi* ille *deus non daretur*, 'as if *that* God did not exist'.

This introduces the great task to which the Council summoned present-day theology: a new conception of God, one that would not only respect the legitimate autonomy of creation but also show it as corresponding to 'the will of the Creator'. This has to be done in such a way that religious consciousness holds both extremes to be true: (a) that human beings live in a world in which 'all things are endowed with their own stability, truth, goodness, proper laws, and order', and (b) that God continues to be the *unum necessarium*.

It is not too bold to state that the whole endeavour of modern theology carries this demand nailed to its innermost being, to the point where this demand makes it possible to interpret the proposals for renovation that mark out its road. This can clearly be seen in the two great movements that have most shaken Christian theology in modern times: Protestant liberalism and Catholic modernism. They did not quite achieve the balance, but both recognized the underlying longing: a *God* who humanized from within and did not rush in from outside; a *revelation* that did not alienate reason but led it to its ultimate roots; a *divine action* that did not take the place of human freedom and actions but supported and empowered them.

This is why perhaps the two greatest disasters of theology in the twentieth century were the Catholic condemnation of modernism and the reaction of Protestant neo-orthodoxy against liberalism. Both contained exaggerations and certainly needed correcting and balancing. But the accusations against them were made – and are still too often made – from the old image of a super-naturalist and interventionist god. Only in this way can the absolute condemnation on grounds of naturalist reductionism made in *Pascendi* or Barth's accusation that this was a way of talking *only* about man and not about God be understood. How much more accurate Barth was when as a historian he warned against 'a widely disseminated opinion in theological circles today' that thought the hand of God had drawn back from the nineteenth century and did not perceive that ultimately his representatives 'were concerned with nothing other than acceptance and confession of Christian revelation'![12]

In the final analysis, it is a matter of re-thinking the relationship between immanence and transcendence. And the decisive problem consists in finding the proper mediation, taking account of the contributions that have been made at various stages, from Schleiermacher's evangelical proposal to Catholic philosophy of immanence or the critical philosophy of ontotheology. The Council raised the idea of creation, speaking of 'reference to [the] Creator' and stating that 'without the Creator, the creature would disappear'. And, in effect, I believe that today the idea of *creation through love* probably supplies the most effective mediation.[13] By speaking of creation, it preserves the maximum difference; by viewing it from love, however, it ensures the greatest identity (greater than that of a mother with her child; Is. 49.15). Founding and upholding the world, God promotes its autonomy without interfering in it, is a living presence without having to 'enter' into a space that is already full of his active presence, with unrestricted and absolute initiative.

Whether or not this diagnosis is totally accurate, Vatican II was certainly moving in this direction. This seals its overall newness and guides its theology on specific points. As I have said, it was not always able to achieve complete coherence. The Council has left present-day theology with the great challenge of accepting its call, gauging the degree to which it carried out its proposals, and progressing toward a more perfect balance.

III. The tasks for present-day theology

The central nature of autonomy undoubtedly provides the best route through the complex terrain of theological concerns. The balance to be struck between the autonomy of each specific field of reality and its constitutive reference to the Creator draws the main lines of the programme and allows us to measure the contribution of the Council. I shall point to three main areas. As is obvious, apart from the fact that any selection to some extent reflects the preferences of its author,[14] the list here is reduced to basics, leaving many questions and many aspects out of consideration.

(1). Taking account of the *autonomy of the individual* certainly forms the most defining and updating impression. It had already made itself felt in the Reformation, with its emphasis on *faith* and on *grace*, with its *pro me* and return to the sources in search of the founding experience, but it has now reached a new maturity.[15]

This is something that made itself felt, from the beginning, in *Dei Verbum*, and why it rejected the previous schema, which was objectivizing and extrinsicist, when it recognized the constitutive implication of human reception for divine revelation itself, with the resultant acceptance of its historical character (one of the Council's great contributions)[16] and of the need for a critical reading of the Bible. This was a decisive breakthrough, even though its implementation was held back by compromises that, as in the case of the 'two sources' or the relationship of scripture, tradition, and magisterium, impeded its progress. There is still an unresolved need for a deepening of the process, based in consistent fashion on a 'theonomous reason' and thereby eliminating the vestiges of supernaturalism that makes inspiration into a sort of psychological 'miracle', particularizes it empirically, so making a real dialogue among religions impossible, and encourages crypto-fundamentalist readings.[17]

The Declaration *Dignitatis humanae*, on religious freedom, belongs, as its title implies, in the same area. Its novelty was emphasized by the strong resistance it had to overcome before being approved. There is still lacking, all the same, a stronger and more decided application of its principles directed within the Church itself. *Moral theology* too experienced an advance, with the ending of casuistry and its organic inclusion in Christian life. But the very fact that the previous schema, prepared in advance, was rejected without another being put in its place shows that we are only at the beginning of one of the great outstanding tasks. We still need to develop a real 'theonomy' that can, on the one hand, uphold the autonomy of moral contents, based on ethical reason and not on religion, while, on the other, preserving their religious integration, by recognizing them as responding identically to the substance of the creature and the loving will of the Creator who founds and sustains them. This would give rise to a greater credibility and would remove the need for many conflicts in the current search, above all in matters of sexuality, health, and bioethics.

(2) The *autonomy of nature* appears in a significantly dual aspect. On principle, it is the most clearly recognized autonomy, as since the crisis over

Galileo it has been the one to make the clearest impression. Natural realities obey internal laws: the moon is not moved by 'angelic forms' (which even Kepler still believed!), plagues are not caused by demons, and the book of Joshua is not competent in astronomical matters. It no longer makes sense to think of divine 'interventionism' in empirical proceedings.[18] Acceptance of this principle, however, is still far from having deployed all its practical consequences. The rejection of deism served as a screen for not heeding its justified call to deny super-natural interferences in the ordering of the world. In place of a revolution that, as Karl Rahner rightly said, should start from the fact that 'God operates *the* world and therefore does not operate *in the* world',[19] what came about was an accommodation, a sort of 'interventionist deism' that, along with deism, accepted that God does not ordinarily interfere but, along with the old supernaturalism, goes on thinking that he does so from time to time.

Neither Vatican II nor subsequent theology in general has really given this problem its due consideration. This has serious consequences, and it is here that one of the most important tasks for the future is emerging, since it affects absolutely fundamental questions that, laden with a heavy interventionist cargo, are seriously distorting the image of God in modern understanding. Let me list some of them:

– Insistence on *miracles*, which would not only break the autonomy of the world but which would also insinuate that God is partial (yes to some, no to others) and that his love is not infinite (before the miracle he had not done all he could do).
– This ties in with *prayer* in its *petition* mode, since, ultimately, this form of praying almost always seeks a divine 'intervention' (to cure illness or strengthen character, to do away with hunger or prevent earthquakes).
– This in turn ties in with the *problem of evil*, since, if it is not interpreted as the inevitable consequence of a finite world (as Leibniz was beginning to see), presents God either as not wishing to intervene or – which is worse – as directly causing the evil. It then becomes honestly impossible to resolve 'the dilemma of Epicurus' (if he does not want to, God is not good; if he wants to, he is not omnipotent): the harm this lack of clarification has produced since the Lisbon earthquake is renewed day by day with each natural disaster and individual misfortune.
– More subtly, perhaps, understanding of the *sacraments* is also implicated afresh: their efficacy is still all too often conceived as a sort of 'invisible miracle' with inevitable magical connotations.
– This also applies to how we understand the *resurrection*, seeking to estab-

lish its objectivity through the 'empty tomb' or, at least, empirical 'apparitions'.

All these are, as can be seen, questions that Vatican II was not able to pursue, but which it does enable us to place under a fresh light. Specifically, the last allusion refers us back to the significant fact that, although it did not work out a *Christology*, it did lay the foundations for the most important renewal that this has undergone in history. Its great success was to have rooted it in humanity: Christ reveals 'through his whole work of making himself present and manifesting himself: through his words and deeds, his signs and wonders, but especially through his death and glorious resurrection' (DV 4a); as a result, 'only in the mystery of the incarnate Word does the mystery of man take on light', since Christ 'fully reveals man to man himself' (GS 22a). In the light of this basic insight, which centres and orientates the whole Christian view of immanence-transcendence relationships, many discussions, such as those that revolve around whether it is better to proceed 'from below' or 'from above', often turn out to be minor skirmishes that distract attention from what is vital.

(3) The *autonomy of the social sphere*, which since the French Revolution has weighed heavily on church consciousness and which met with strong resistance on account of its collision with ruling interests (the official pronouncements of the nineteenth century today cause painful consternation), was one of the great steps forward taken by the Council. *Gaudium et spes* took it by looking toward the *world*. This explains its success and its favourable reception, to the point where we might say that its impulse brought about the updating – the most consistent achieved to date – of a major theological dimension: the social efficacy of a gospel that proclaims 'Blessed are the poor' and of a 'faith working through love' (Gal. 5.6). This is what – beyond subjects of secondary importance – political theologies of liberation have made clear. This is not always understood by those who accuse them of ingenuousness or optimism, who, instead of looking at the Council's act of basic acceptance (necessary and widely expected), concentrate on the letter of some concrete applications.

For its part, *Lumen gentium* initiated this process looking within *the Church*, through its rightly called 'Copernican revolution', proclaiming that the Church's ultimate reality lies in the fraternal community of all believers as 'people of God', and situating the various offices, including the hierarchical one, only within this. The unfortunate thing was that, in the concern to establish episcopal collegiality, this was isolated from that of the whole Church, narrowing it into a juridical and hierarchizing concept.[20]

As early as 1970, Cardinal Suenens was saying that 'the future of the Church will depend' on a re-equilibration of this matter.[21] And in strict adherence to the gospel – 'But it is not so among you; but whoever wishes to become great among you must be your servant, and whoever wishes to be first among you must be slave of all' (see Mark 10.42–5 par.) – it has to be admitted that an appropriate 'democratization' is necessary for the life of the Church. Those who do not like the word or even mistrust the symbol 'people of God' can replace them with others such as 'communion' or 'synodality',[22] but disagreements over names should not obscure the question of real values: if not a 'democracy' in the political sense, the Church can never be less than a democracy in the true sense.

With regard to the *base of the Church*, this is urgently in need of a revitalization of egalitarian communion, doing away with the scandalous circumstance – in modern consciousness – that in the Church all deliberations should have only a consultative character, and, of course, bringing in full equality of *women*, thereby redeeming, against all historical inertia, the shining and foundational Pauline principle that in Christ 'there is no longer male and female' (Gal. 3.28).

And with regard to *hierarchical government*, the autonomy of society forces us to undertake an honest and forceful rethinking of the divine origin of authority, parallel to that done for civil authority (to which Romans 13.1–2 referred in the first place!), showing that this does not prevent it from being founded, transmitted, elected, and defended through the community. In this sense it is, for example, illuminating to read what *Pacem in terris* said of civil society and apply it to the Church: 'The fact that authority comes from God does not mean that men have no power to choose those who are to rule the State [or Church], or to decide upon the type of government they want, and determine the procedure and limitations of rulers in their exercise of their authority. Hence the above teaching is consonant with any genuinely democratic form of government.'[23]

Given the present speeding-up of historical development and the worldwide spread of the Church, nether should we draw back from the appropriateness of setting time limits on offices, as being the best way of keeping to the principle of the *ecclesia semper reformanda*: the pastoral efficacy of this has been proved by the religious orders over centuries, and its theological legitimacy is included in the introduction of a retirement age of seventy-five for bishops.

IV. Opening out

Other basic diagnoses and so other choices of subjects are obviously possible. Those listed above however do concern real problems and indicate urgent tasks. Two very important subjects still need to be added: they are made more so by very fact of having celebrated the most universal of all councils.

The first is a new *ecumenical consciousness*. This is obviously true in respect of the Christian confessions, whose differences are increasingly looking like domestic squabbles, which, as Karl Rahner and Heinrich Fries pointed out,[24] could be resolved now with generous respect for differences. And it is extending unstoppably toward the other religions: the Council was timid here, since although it recognized positive values in them, it did not dare to state clearly that they too possess values that are strictly religious and revealed.[25] But it did open and sanction a door on to one of the most decisive areas of current religious thinking.

Something similar happened with the *problem of atheism*. There was a move from polemical condemnation to recognition that believers have 'more than a little to do with the birth of atheism' (GS 19) and acceptance of its positive contributions, to the point where *fuga mundi* is now supplanted by positive appreciation of its autonomy, and *'extra ecclesiam nulla salus'* has been replaced by the new perception, well expressed some time ago by H. Zahrnt and popularized by Schillebeeckx, that 'outside the world there is no salvation'.[26]

So, to sum up: the task of a theology that, without being bound by the letter of Vatican II, seeks to put its spirit into effect consists in collecting together the elements of renewal arising from the Reformation and later attempts at responding to the cultural shift brought about by modernity.[27] At its heart there must be a concern to spell out afresh the autonomy of the world and the revelation of a God who creates out of love and who 'is love' (1 John 4.8, 16). A God who, therefore, is not and seeks not anything other than salvation for his creatures. A God who, in the inaugural words of the new pope, 'takes nothing away and gives everything' and who, in an accurate translation of St Anselm's saying, loves us with 'a greater love than we can think of.'[28]

Translated by Paul Burns

Notes

1. Hans Küng, *Christianity: Its Essence* (London and New York 1995), ch. 3.
2. Cf. e.g., 'Vatican II et son héritage' in M. Lambergist and L. Kenis (eds), *Vatican II and Its Legacy* (Louvain 2002), pp. 1–24, here p. 1.

3. *The Origin and Goal of History*, New York 1977.
4. 'Neues Testament und Mythologie' in H. W. Bartsch (ed.), *Kerygma und Mythos*, Hamburg 1948, p. 18; see 'Zum Problem der Entmthyologisierung' in *Glauben und Vestehen IV*, Tübingen 1967, pp. 128–37; *Jesus Christ and Mythology*, London 1960.
5. Karl Barth, *Die protestantische Theologie im 19. Jaherhundert*, Zurich 1960, p, 15. In fact one would all too often have to say *very* outdated. There could be no harm in re-reading the trustworthy evidence of this book to revive an understanding of this pressure.
6. Paul Brand, 'Church and Theology', *Concilium* (1970), *The Future of the Church*.
7. 'The Opening Speech', *ibid*.
8. Alfons Auer aptly observes that 'at this point the Council tries to overturn a deep bitterness in modern man' ('Das Zweite Vatikanische Konzil, III', *LThK*, 1986, p. 385).
9. This at least is the viewpoint adopted here; see more detailed discussions in P. Gisel and P. Evrard (eds), *La théologie en postmodernité*, Geneva 1996.
10. I refer her to my *Fin del cristianismo premoderno*, Santander 2000.
11. Einstein, for example, could not accept a personal God, because he *always assumed* that this would eliminate the autonomy of physical laws: this is the meaning of his well known phrase, 'God does not play dice'. But the *theological* solution cannot be found on the level of *physical science*, arguing from 'indeterminism' (cf., e.g., data and discussion in D. Hattrup, 'O Deus de Einstein, afinal, joga aos dados', *Revista Poruguesa de Filosofia* 61 [2005], pp. 113–28; the whole issue is important in this respect).
12. *Op. cit.* (n. 5 above), p. 13.
13. I have tried to show this in my *Recuperar la creación*, Santander ³2001).
14. I apologize for what might seem a dogmatic tone in such a brief summary, but my remarks stem from a long concern with these matters: see Biog. Note.
15. Troeltsch's thesis on the not yet modern character of the Reformation can be refined in detail, but its basic thesis is true on any assessment: *Die Bedeutung des Protestantismus für die Enstehung der Moderne*, Munich and Berlin 1925.
16. On the subject of chapter 2 and its acceptance of the historicity of tradition, Luis Alonso Schökel has stated, 'This second chapter is perhaps the most important contribution made by the Constitution, and, seen from the future, it may be seen as the most important of the whole Council. The reason is that it does not stop at moving forward in one particular section but proclaims the principle of progress as constitutive of the Church': 'El dinamismo de la tradición' in *Idem* (ed.), *Comentarios a la Constitución* Dei Verbum *sobre la divina revelación*, Madrid 1969, p. 228.
17. It is strange that Barth's reasonable protest on relationship to the magisterium, in which he goes so far as to speak of the Council having a 'fainting fit' or even 'heart attack' ('Conciliorum Tridentiniet Vaticani inhaerens vestigiis?' in B. D.

Dupuy [ed.], *Vaticano II. La Revelación Divina*, Madrid 1970, p. 234), should be allied, on the other hand, with an inconsistent reserve on this last point. In his conversations in Rome with Rahner, Semmelroth, and Ratzinger he advised them that the Catholic Church should refrain from following, as the Protestant Churches had done, the philosophies that became fashionable from the seventeenth century onward: see S. Madrigal, *Memoria del Concilio. Diez evocaciones del Vaticano II*, Madrid–Bilbao 2005, p. 284.
18. The account by N. M. Wildiers, *Weltbild und Theologie*, Zurich–Einsiedeln–Cologne 1974, remains valid and eloquent, showing the depth and difficulty of the process: 'Throughout the seventeenth century theology remained [. . .] tied to the medieval representation of the universe' (p. 262) and what was taught in seminaries and faculties 'was a monotonous and precarious cast of what the great masters of the thirteenth century had taught' (p. 266).
19. *Grundkurs des Glaubens*, Freiburg 1976, p. 94: 'dass Gott *die* Welt wirkt und nicht eigentlich *in die* Welt'.
20. In this volume Giuseppe Alberigo notes that there was no 'conciliarism' in the Fathers, but there is on the other hand no denying that there were traces of 'papalism', such as the Prefatory Note added to *Lumen gentium* ('from a higher authority there is communicated to the Fathers . . .') or the fact that some subjects were reserved to the Pope by being withdrawn from conciliar discussion.
21. *Loc. cit.*, p. 185.
22. See A. Melloni and S. Scatena (eds), *Synod and Synodality*, Bologna 2005.
23. Vatican II accepted the same idea: 'It is therefore obvious that the political community and public authority are based on human nature and hence belong to an order of things divinely foreordained' (GS 74d). For the classic texts see B. Schwalm, 'Democratie', *DThC* 4 (1939), pp. 271–321, esp. 289–93; see also E. Valton, 'État', *DThC* 5 (1939), pp. 875905, esp. 887–90; A. Bride, 'Tyranni, tyrannicide', *DThC* 15 (1950), pp. 1948–98, esp. 1953–66.
24. H. Fries and K. Rahner, *Union of the Churches: an actual possibility*, Philadelphia 1985.
25. Cf. especially NA 2.
26. H. Zahrnt, *Die Sache mit Gott*, Munich 1966, p. 162; E. Schillebeeckx, *Los hombres, relato de Dios*, Salamanca 1994, pp. 29–41, 248.
27. Schleiermacher's approach is almost always exemplary in such cases. It is well summed up by Tillich: 'In the development of each thought attend first to orthodox theology, then to pietistic critique of orthodoxy, and finally to Enlightenment critique of both tendencies, before proposing your own solution' (*Vorlesungen über die Geschichte des christlichen Denkens* I, Stuttgart 1971, p. 291).
28. Schelling had made the application in reference to revelation: see e.g. *Philosophie der Offenbarung* I, Darmstadt 1974, p. 27; a good study of the subject is J. Werbick, *Den Glauben verantworten. Eine Fundamentaltheologie*, Freiburg–Basle–Vienna 2000, pp. 286–89 and *passim*.

II. Vatican II Today?: What is its Core?

'The Others': Ecumenism and Religions

MAURO VELATI

A few months after the announcement of the Council in 1959, the theologian Yves Congar posed the question of the relationship between the Church and Christians with 'others', reading the seeds of an opening out in the signs of the times: 'This new awareness of the existence of 'Others', this need to take an interest in them, is one of the most characteristic traits of the present generation of Christians.'[1] In debates within Christendom 'the other' could only be 'the dissident'. The time for recognizing other spiritual worlds was then imminent, nonetheless. In various ways the Council embodied this need, not only in separate statements in its teaching but in its whole dawning self-confidence. The Council was an internal function of Catholicism, but it followed in the wake of John XXIII's teaching, and he had indicated that its charismatic aspect (the 'new Pentecost') depended on its openness to a new understanding of the Church itself. This does not exist for itself but as '*lumen gentium*', 'a kind of sacrament or sign of intimate union with God, and of the unity of all mankind' (LG 1b). Today – forty years on – the need is still with us even if the historical circumstances have changed profoundly.

Congar in his article drew attention to the conditions of pluralism that were already beginning to characterize European society to a significant extent, and he lingered over the existence of various 'spiritual worlds' (non-Catholic denominations but also other religions and the world of atheism and non-belief). Today the panorama of the Christian world has changed with the crisis of mainstream denominations and the spread of Pentecostal groups, autonomous churches in Africa and Latin America, and sects that keep a more or less vague reference to Christian roots. The rise of Islam in Western societies and the new scenario of the 'clash of civilizations' have produced a new definition of relations with what is now the second largest world religion in terms of adherents. What was formerly the intuition of small groups and individuals particularly sensitive to the 'Abrahamitic' origins of the three monotheistic religions has now become a more than spiritual necessity. Our relationship with materialism has also been placed in an entirely new setting, not ideological but against the backdrop of globalization of consumption and a now widespread homogenization of culture.

I. Unity among Christians

The sector of Christian ecumenism has been the one to show the most rapid and eventful development in relations in the years of the Council and after. For several decades the Catholic world had shown a lively concern for the comparisons brought out by the ecumenical movement, as the lives of the pioneers (Beaudoin, Congar, Villain, Willebrands and others) demonstrate. The World Council of Churches in Geneva had prepared an effective contribution, providing stimulus and pressure, to the preparation for the Council. The conciliar decree fully recognized the value of the ecumenical process, negating the condemnations from the time of Pius XI (*Mortalium animos*). The presence of the observers in Rome during the Council furnished the basis for an entirely new experience of communion, which was in some measure to be continued with the formation of mixed commissions for bilateral discussions. The possibility of integrating the Catholic Church fully in the structure of the World Council in Geneva was seriously considered a few years after the Council, even though it was never finally approved.[2]

Like all great processes of change, this too would need a much longer time span than forty years for a historical evaluation to be made. Only over the long term is it possible to grasp the deep changes the Council primed, not only on the level of Catholic theology but also in the very life of the Church, in spirituality as well as in catechesis. Ecumenical considerations became one component among others in Catholic culture, thanks to the spread of capillary initiatives, among which the Week of Prayer for Christian Unity naturally stands out. This is now an established tradition and, unlike in the first years of the Council, is increasingly becoming an occasion of true meetings of Christians from different denominations. Perception of others is no longer mediated through the rigidity of canon law categories (heretics and schismatics) but through acceptance of a common Christian heritage much more generally felt nowadays. For the generation before the Council, non-Catholics were at best granted to be in 'good faith', in much the same manner as believers of other religions. Today acceptance of diversity in worship and in forms of church organization among different Christian traditions is general even in countries with a Catholic majority. And among most Christians the ecclesial reality of the separated communities is generally accepted *de facto* – while it is still being discussed by theologians and the magisterium. The different forms taken by conciliar renewal in various fields of the life of the Church (laity, religious life, catechesis) reflect these changes, involving a fundamental concern for others that soon became daily practice and communion. We have the example of new movements that quite often cross confessional boundaries, not to mention monastic ways of life in which their spirituality reflects an effective recovery of the traditions of the undivided Church.

On the institutional level the mixed commissions and discussion groups are not the only instruments of conciliar renewal. On the local level, Catholicism has absorbed the application of ecumenism through the formation of diocesan commissions and also of church councils at district, regional, or national level. It is precisely on these levels that ecumenical dynamism is often stronger than at the top. The popular consciousness of modern society has even embraced ecumenical events, giving them a previously unheard-of degree of mass visibility. The annual gatherings of the Taizé Community bring together young people from a wide variety of national and confessional backgrounds. The Graz Assembly of 1997, planned as a meeting of delegates from the European Churches, turned into a genuine 'people's' gathering, a festival of meeting and reconciliation. This is no longer the ecumenism of church history manuals, of small groups of pioneers, but of gatherings that have become structural, or at least have acquired continuity.

The road taken by Catholicism has joined an already existing way (the historic ecumenism of the WCC), but it has made its own special contributions, not without producing tensions and problems. The contribution made by the popes to ecumenism is an element that it would be very hard to overvalue. It has played a principal role in the events of the last forty years. It has been a constant notion in the pontificates of recent years that the Pope himself has a role to play in overcoming divisions, simply through his – sometimes dramatic – understanding that he is one of the principal causes of them. Pope Paul VI expressed this well when he addressed the WCC Assembly in Geneva in 1969: 'Our name is Peter [. . . and] We are convinced that the Lord has granted Us, without any merit on Our part, a ministry of communion. He has certainly not given Us this charism in order to isolate Us from you, nor to exclude from among us understanding, collaboration, brotherhood, and finally composition of unity, but rather to leave Us the precept and the gift of love, in truth and in humility.'[3]

The popes from John XXIII to the present have viewed their own place in the ecumenical sphere not only in relation to the authority conferred on them by their office but increasingly also in terms of personal witness and endeavour. They have accordingly imbued aspects of this with a strong personal flavour. John XXIII was the charismatic pope of personal relations, open to viewing non-Catholics as 'brothers', united in discovering a common religious and sacramental heritage. He furthered a process, through convoking the Council, even though he did not see its outcome and did not try to manage its complex dynamics. Paul VI is remembered as the pope of ecumenical gestures, who tried through symbolism to move beyond the limits imposed by divergent theological and ecclesiological outlooks. He found himself having to manage probably the most difficult phase, in which pointers from the Council and above all the 'leap forward' of the experience of communion the Council had provided needed to find a concrete means of insertion into the body of Catholicism. At a time when ecumenical euphoria was being welded with displays of youthful rebelliousness – a phenomenon that has still not been adequately studied on the historical level – Paul VI had a dramatic feeling of concern over a loss of the sense of Catholic traditions in the context of ecumenical openness.

The long pontificate of John Paul II was probably the full term of building a post-conciliar Catholicism. He several times reaffirmed the irreversibility of the ecumenical drive of the Catholic Church and underscored this in the first encyclical in the history of the papacy to be expressly devoted to the promotion of unity through ecumenism, *Ut unum sint* of 1995. John Paul II brought a very personal style to ecumenical relationships, in which the value of visits and meetings was set above that of institutional aspects. New features of the ecumenical experience were prized as a result of historical readings typical of the pope: such was the case of the link between ecumenism and martyrdom just hinted at in *Lumen gentium* 15: 'Some [non-Catholic Christians] indeed He has strengthened to the extent of shedding of their blood'. This legacy has been placed at the apex of the historical course of the past century and celebrated right at the centre of the year 2000, after being set out in *Ut unum sint* 48: 'Is not the twentieth century a time of great witness, which extends "even to the shedding of blood"?'. The 1986 Assisi meeting was another example of creative reworking of the Council's intuitions. This produced contrasting reactions: on one side traditionalist fears of the supposed adoption of forms of syncretism; on the other criticisms of 'staginess' and the fears of many Christians of a sort of papal monopoly on interfaith dialogue. Beyond all this, nevertheless, the occasion did seem to point to the way of enabling ecumenical dialogue to escape from a downward spiral of closure and of progressive bureaucratization. In this sense, ecumenism is not diminished but rather strengthened through being inserted in a wider context, in which people's longings for peace converge with varying manifestations of religious belief.

These are indications of changes that have their time and that naturally require a continuous stimulus and reference to the original motivations. Against the background of these changes the parabola of post-conciliar ecumenism has over these forty years traced its course of advance and retreat, with unforeseen slowdowns and accelerations. We have become used to speaking of a period of 'euphoria' (to the end of the 1960s), followed by disappointment, the 'ecumenical winter'. The ecumenical endeavour has a precise and demanding objective: visible unity among Christians. This can certainly be interpreted on various levels, from a purely spiritual unity that leaves structural variations intact to a true and proper visible 'unification' of the Churches, of which partial examples are not lacking in the history of the ecumenical movement. Full unification, though, remains the absolute reference point against which partial gains must be measured from time to time. This is the root of the 'critical' (in the sense of always being exposed to crisis) nature of the ecumenical endeavour. At least in Catholic circles in the years immediately following the Council, there was never a moment when someone was not talking of the 'crisis' of ecumenism, even with the obvious evidence of a process that was moving forward.

Today this situation is viewed with greater disappointment. Acknowledgement that we have – in some ways – gone down a 'blind alley' should not exempt us from seeking new ways to an 'Ecumenical Constitution of Churches',[4] even if ecumenism today looks '[...] more like the management of present diversities than like a rapid process of unification among the Churches'.[5] There is no doubt than even the most representative body of the ecumenical movement, the World Council of Churches, is today visibly in its own crisis and looking for a 'reconfiguration' of its own profile, as well as an institutional restructuring.[6] Many things have happened. Non-theological factors such as the historical developments in Eastern Europe have profoundly altered the position of the Orthodox Churches and their relationship with Catholicism. The question of proselytism has once again come to the fore and is now the critical point, despite numerous conferences devoted to the subject and the Catholic–Orthodox Balamand Agreement. Questions long discussed in past theological meetings are coming back, sometimes with a critical force that seems to obliterate the lines of achieved consensus. The actual decisions taken at church summits in the doctrinal and pastoral fields do not always take account of possible relapses on the ecumenical level.

II. The 'people [. . .] most dear' in Lumen gentium 16

Dialogue with the Jewish world – like that with other religions – has not had the support of an organized movement comparable to the ecumenical movement, though it has benefited from the friendship between many Jews and Christians. The actual story of the inclusion of this subject in the conciliar agenda is rather remarkable: it originated with the visit by Jules Isaacs and the decision by Pope John XXIII to ask Cardinal Bea and his Secretariat for Christian Unity to study the matter – a conjunction of occasional factors whose outcome could not be discounted. What stands out in the story however is the dialogical nature of the conciliar event itself, which – following the indications set out by Pope John – became an arena open to pleas from the world outside, from the 'others', indeed. Complicated as it was by significant historical factors (the weight of the Catholic tradition of anti-Jewish feeling, the shadow of the Holocaust, the arguments just starting over the actions of Pius XII), the question had a difficult passage through the Council, eventually producing its outcome in section 4 of *Nostra Aetate*. This, nevertheless, went beyond the expectations of many, in that – as Brockway notes – from the angle of replacing the theology of substitution and of re-reading the biblical texts on the position of Israel in relation to Christianity, this text overtook the positions adopted by the Churches gathered at WCC Assemblies, from Evanston in 1954 to New Delhi in 1961.[7] Furthermore, it provided a valid alternative to the 'unionistic' approach expressed in seeking personal conversions. It is well known that in both Catholic and Protestant circles consolidation of the process of assimilating Judaism in Western countries, from the beginning of the last century, had opened the doors to the dream of a final re-absorption of the Jewish religion into Christianity.

The text of *Nostra Aetate* proved to be the starting point for a movement that has known its times of crisis and retreat, becoming entangled in often mischievous polemics on the Church's attitude to Nazi anti-Semitism during the Second World War. Here too the fury of polemic often veils an underlying reality that, over the long time span of reception, has itself changed profoundly. The theological discussion has moved beyond the insights of the Council, which many people judged still to bear traces of the theology of substitution. Ecclesiology too is trying to develop the central point to emerge during the Council – even though its expression remained summary – of the indissoluble link between the Church's understanding of itself and its relation to its Hebrew roots.[8] The two documents produced by the Commission for religious Relations with the Jews, 'Guidelines and Suggestions for Implementing the Conciliar Declaration *Nostra Aetate* (no. 4)' in 1974 and 'Notes on the Correct Way to Present the Jews and Judaism in Preaching and Catechism in the Roman Catholic Church' in 1985,[9] demonstrate – even allowing for the obvious limitations of each – a concern to take forward a series of matters that the Council, for various reasons, had not been able to develop, from Isaacs' original request for a correction to Christian teaching on the Jews to revision of some aspects of Catholic liturgy and devotions.

The subject has however always been bedevilled with historical and political factors. At the Council the greatest opposition to the approval of *Nostra Aetate* came from Arab Christian and from Vatican diplomats fearful that it would lead to a worsening of relations with Middle Eastern countries. Later, however, the political debate produced a swing in the opposite direction. The opening of diplomatic relations between Israel and the Holy See with the General Agreement of 1993 has proved a powerful stimulus to dialogue, on the strictly religious as well as political front. The Holy See has tried to keep the two aspects separate (for example by underlining the 'Religious Relations' in the Commission's title), but crossovers are probably inevitable, in view of the actual conditions of present-day Judaism. One important factor is that the diplomats on both sides (from the Israeli Embassy in Rome and the Apostolic Nunciature in Jerusalem) take part of right in the strictly religious parts of discussions, according to a formula that must be unique in the field of interfaith dialogue.

Pope John Paul II made a characteristic contribution on this question, emphasizing and deepening the meaning of the link between the Church and the Hebrew people, in line with the Council's original insight. From John XXIII's 'I am John, your brother!', through the appeal to 'elder brethren' during John Paul's visit to the Rome synagogue, there has been a continuity *in crescendo*, culminating, in more than a symbolic sense, in the latter's visit to Jerusalem in 2000. Today there are areas of dialogue and discussion where various religious sensitivities have been brought together through common action. In the sphere of the Committee for Catholic–Jewish Relations, whose eighteen meetings (from 1970 to 2004) now make up a small *corpus* of reference work, discussion has concentrated on ethical-religious themes, moving from a first phase of mutual clarification of relations in the past to a second phase of common endeavour in tackling the major problems of the world today. The most recent encounter between the Chief Rabbinate of Israel and the Vatican Commission has developed along the same lines. Of course we cannot here speak of theological dialogue in the sense of the ecumenical tradition. As Geoffrey Wigoder has written: 'On theological points, we are looking for understanding, not agreement.'[10] Themes such as the value of human life or the family nevertheless provide the territory on which religious people can meditate together from the basis of their own traditions. And reference to common religious roots finds its own congruous space within this dialogue, as was shown in the progress of the third meeting (1–3 Dec. 2003 in Jerusalem) between the delegates of the Chief Rabbinate and the Vatican Commission, on the subject of 'The Relevance of Central Teachings in the Holy Scriptures which we share for Contemporary Society and the Education of Future Generations accordingly'. This was not so much a matter of an alliance between religions against the common enemy of materialism (as it had often been branded in the last century) as an encounter at the very roots of faith itself.

Relations with the Jewish world – the 'sacrament of otherness', as it has been described[11] – are still an exposed nerve for the Churches and for Western society, and seen in this way it is clear that the process brought about by the Council is still at the development stage. The 'eternal return' of polemic over the silences of Pius XII, the resurgence of more of less disguised forms of anti-Semitism, interference from *parti-pris* pronouncements of the Catholic magisterium that not only Jewish public opinion finds hard to understand as they are expressed (*Dominus Deus* being the most obvious example): these are just some of the examples of crises that have emerged in the last few years.

III. The world religions

The subject of dialogue with other religions arose in the Council in a fairly casual manner. Not that sensitivity on this point was lacking in some Catholic circles. Among the *vota* sent by bishops and theological faculties on the eve of the Council, there were some expressing the need for a prepared view on relations with Islam and the Eastern religions. Most of the bishops however were mainly concerned with relations within Catholicism and did not regard interfaith dialogue as a priority. The need to preserve the much-discussed document on the Jews then decided the introduction of the subject at the Council. Cardinal Cicognani's '*Si de Judaeis, cur not etiam de Mahumedanis?*', a strategic move by an ex-diplomat, brought about a change, very soon attracting the livelier elements in Catholicism.

Dialogue with other religions was not underpinned by a pioneering tradition, as the ecumenical movement was. There was no existing equivalent of the Protestant WCC among the world religions. Even within the ecumenical movement attention to the religions was often overlaid with the imperative of mission. It was symptomatic that only in the 1970s did the WCC first devote a session to dialogue with 'people of living faiths and ideologies'.[12] The great initiators of dialogue with Islam (L. Massignon and Fr Gardet) and with Eastern religions (J. Monchanin and H. Le Saux) were somewhat isolated figures, though influential at times. The actual birth of the Secretariat for Non-Christians (1964), effected by Paul VI on the back of his vision of concentric circles elaborated in *Ecclesiam Suam*, was deliberately given a very low profile, to the extent that some outside observers called it – perhaps a little unkindly – 'the Non-Secretariat for Dialogue with Non-Christians'. Also, religious dialogue is a complex process. The objectives, it must be said, were not very clear, and the general approach was not aimed – as ecumenical dialogue was – at achieving full unity. In this field the variety of approaches and of categories hides the very possibility of truly understanding other parties. Furthermore, there was a lack of institutional reference-point to fall back on. Cardinal Pignedoli, the long-serving head of the Secretariat for Dialogue, summed up the meaning of the work done in these words: 'We have limited ourselves to the service of friendship toward our non-Christian brethren. This friendship is religious, based on eternal spiritual values.' The progress of interfaith dialogue is far from the mature reconciliations of intra-Christian ecumenism.

In this field too there was a need to settle accounts with the legacy of the past. Catholicism had often regarded the worlds of the other religions as competitors or as open spaces for Christian evangelization. Christianity itself had often shown itself to these worlds under the mantle of colonialism. Penetrating the Asian world had been one of the great challenges in the history of Christianity, but by the eve of the Council its achievements could only be regarded as modest, with the notable exception of some countries with a strong Catholic presence. The Council began the season of dialogue with a renewal of missiology and the extension of dialogue to include non-Christian religions, but it needed to define relations with 'others' more precisely and to reconcile the opposing requirements of evangelizing mission and respect for the religious patrimony of others. *Nostra Aetate* had already brought these two aspects together, leaving the mission demand open: 'The Catholic Church rejects nothing which is true and holy in these religions. She looks with sincere respect upon those ways of conduct and of life, those rules and teachings which, though differing in many particulars from what she holds and sets forth, nevertheless often reflect a ray of light of the Truth which enlightens all men. Indeed, she proclaims and must ever proclaim Christ, "the way, the truth and the life" (John 14.6), in whom all men find the fullness of religious life, and in whom God has reconciled all things to himself (cf. 2 Cor. 5.19–19)' (NA 2e). It was on this point – far more than on the condemnation of anti-Semitism – that the traditionalist bishops of the *Coetus* concentrated their criticisms on the eve of the final vote on *Nostra Aetate*.

This is also the point on which theological debate over the last forty years has been focused, not without conflicts and accusations from the opposed critiques of 'relativism' and 'absolutism'. Starting with Karl Rahner, theology has given varying and often contradictory answers between these two extremes. Twenty years ago, in the pages of *Concilium*, Hans Küng put forward an alternative way between the absolutist-exclusivist and the relativist-inclusivist positions, which he defined as a 'critical ecumenical position'. This is a return – more in form than in content – to the original attitude of the pioneers of the ecumenical movement: '[...] remaining faithful to their own faith communities, these succeeded in modifying both themselves and the others, and thereby, over the passage of time, both changing the ecclesial communities.'[13] The Secretariat's formulation is expressed in the 1991 document on 'Dialogue and Proclamation', which – far from closing the debate – has rather tried to propose an intermediate line, firmly maintaining the uniqueness of Christ as mediator of salvation and esteem for the great religious founders.[14]

Leaving aside theological disagreements – which have often produced tensions with deeply wounding results, as in the case of the late lamented Fr Dupuis – dialogue has moved forward through reciprocal encounters and sharing common concerns, areas in which John Paul II provided considerable stimulus. His intuition at the Assisi meeting in 1986 combined rejection of any form of syncretism – which many had feared when the gathering was announced – with common working for peace, not in the form of an ecumenical congress but in the more properly religious one of prayer. This inclusion of the subject of dialogue in a historical setting, open to the dramas of the world and its peoples, was later proved truly far-sighted in the light of the political transformations of the last decades following the end of the Cold War and the prospect of a clash of civilizations, aggravated since 11 September 2001.

In the teaching of John Paul II dialogue among religions is no longer separated from concern for people and the role of religions in open conflicts in various parts of the world. Might we say that in this *Nostra Aetate* is seen in the light of *Gaudium et spes*? The Pope himself often quoted its text concerning the action of the Holy Spirit in human lives: 'For, since Christ died for all men, and since the ultimate vocation of man is in fact one, and divine, we ought to believe that the Holy Spirit in a manner known only to God offers to every man the possibility of being associated with this paschal mystery' (GS 22g). A large part of his efforts at dialogue was unfurled during his apostolic visits, in direct contact with local situations. 'In a world that desires unity and peace and that still knows a thousand tensions and conflicts, should believers not favour friendship and union between all persons and within the people that make up a single community on earth?', he asked young Muslims in Casablanca in 1985. John Paul II's engagement against the most recent international conflicts is largely the synthesis of two primary requirements: the value of peace on one side but also the need to keep dialogue with the Muslim world open on the other.

IV. The Council: living under the eye of the other

The dimension of otherness is still there – and has probably become more complex – in Benedict XVI's view of Catholicism. While differences internal to the historic Churches of East and West are lessening, new concerns requiring full-time attention by the Churches are arising. Catholicism's capacity for making syntheses between universality and particularity, between absolutism of principles and openness to diversity, is being put to the test. This is the real challenge of the reception of Vatican II, now proceeding in a Church henceforth almost completely orphaned of the protagonists of that event but ever more firmly moulded by the pastoral directives it laid down.

The new Pope carries the legacy of his predecessor on his shoulders and clearly cannot limit himself to repeating his gestures and attitudes. The ambivalence of the present moment resides in the possibility of putting flesh on the situations of dialogue started on John Paul II's personal initiative. Will the Churches find means of moving beyond theological-institutional barriers? Today people are willing to return to reflection on spiritual ecumenism, and it is not fortuitous – in the Year of the Eucharist – that the new pope has launched a clear appeal to the Eastern Churches to open up a way toward Eucharistic communion.

More united Christians can re-position themselves to provide a more satisfactory approach to discussions concerning the Jewish matrix, in accordance with the approach suggested by Barth shortly after the Council. Only patient work of building unity among Christians will lead to their being able properly to relate to Israel, and so to the 'fundamental' question of ecumenism. This approach may well bring about the fall both of individual Churches' claims to hegemony and the entrenched political positions that, in the delicate interplay of religious and political factors always present in such matters, have been so obvious in the question of the Middle East. This is also the key for re-undertaking a less fragmentary dialogue among religions, one that no longer be torn between the media-directed dimension of the 'great event' and the need for specificity. More closely united Christians will undoubtedly be able to establish a more authentic dialogue with the world of other religions.

There is general agreement today on the strategic value of this challenge. Yet the importance of the endeavour cannot hide the difficulties and the lack of a shared vision among the Christian Churches themselves. One of the presidents of the WCC, Aram I, has recently stated as much: '[Interfaith] dialogue remains the most complex and most controversial dimension of the ecumenical movement'.[15] There is not only the tendency in some Christian circles to view dialogue as the sphere of a new 'long-term ecumenism'; there are also divergent theological views and differing ways of understanding dialogue: on one side are the defenders of a specifically 'religious' approach; on the other those who favour a practical collaboration of the great socio-political questions of the modern world. Geneva too is feeling a persistent tension between the need to move to a more communitarian dimension of dialogue, no longer reserved to experts, and that of better coordination among the initiatives of individual Churches, which are often disconnected and contradictory.[16]

The world of this beginning of the twenty-first century is in some ways far removed from that of the 1960s, in which the Council opened. The political and religious figures are different, and the dimension of human life itself has changed. This does not mean there is no point in turning back to the spirit and the demands of that time. This is how Congar described the task facing the Council Fathers on the eve of the opening of the Council: 'It will be necessary for all those who work for the Council to have the will to carry out their task as though they were morally under the eye of 'the Others'. Then, indeed, the Council will be able to be the occasion for a fresh approach.'[17] The French theologian's foresight – amply put into effect during the conciliar experience – still remains as a task for today: to live conscious of the 'eye' of others (who are now not primarily out brethren in other denominations), not so as to pass judgment on them but in Christian understanding and love.

Translated by Paul Burns

Notes

1. Y. Congar, 'Le Concile, l'Église et . . . "les Autres"', *Lumière et vie* 45 (1959), p. 74.
2. J. Grootaers, *Rome et Genève á la croisée des chemins (1968–1972)*, Paris 2000.
3. *Insegnamenti del Santo Padre Paulo VI*, VII, pp. 398–401.
4. This is the title of a recent volume of *Concilium*, 2001/3, which starts from the necessary 'de-dramatization' of doctrinal differences in order to establish an ecumenical constitution for the Church, intended 'to make evident, precisely in respect of the ordered whole of the elements that constitute the life of the Church, God's intention, manifested in Jesus of Nazareth, that we all may all be one . . . .'
5. A. Riccardi, *Intransigenze e modernità. La Chiesa cattolica verso il terzo millennio*, Rome–Bari 1996, p. 97.
6. See, *inter alia*, the debate in 'Reconfiguration. Neugestaltung der ökumenischen Bewegung' *Oekumenische Rundschau* 1 (2005), with articles by Aram I, Konrad Raiser, Fritz Eric, W. Thönissen, Wolgang Bienert, and Joachim Willems.
7. A. Broackway, 'Assemblies of the World Council of Churches', in *The Theology of the Churches and the Jewish People*, Geneva 1988, pp. 123–40.
8. This is a point that still needs investigation, together with overall renewal of all theological method, according to Peter Hünermann, in 'La teologia doppo la Nostra Aetate', *Il Regno* 3 (2005), pp. 72–7.
9. Both texts are available in English at www.ewtn.com/library/CURIA/RRJJEWS [trans.].
10. In *Documentation Catholique* 1988, p. 700.
11. A. Melloni, *Chiesa madre, chiesa matrigna*, Turin 2004, p. 55.
12. J. H. Pranger, *Dialogue in Discussion. The WCC and the Challenge of Religious Plurality, 1967–1979*, Utrecht–Leiden 1995.
13. H. Küng, 'Toward an Ecumenical Theology of Religions', in *Concilium* 1986/1.
14. There is an overview of the debate in more recent years, allied to the proposal for a 'kairological approach' as a means of moving beyond exclusivist, inclusivist and parallelist positions, in A. Houtepen, 'Truth Enlightening All People. Christianity and Religious Pluralism after Vatican II', in *Vatican II and Its Legacy*, ed. M. Lamberigts and L. Kenis, Louvain 2002, pp. 207–32.
15. Report by Aram I to the Central Committee of the WCC, Antelias (Lebanon), Aug. 2003.
16. The international conference held in Geneva from 7 to 9 June 2005, on 'A critical moment for interfaith dialogue', with the participation of a delegation from the Pontifical Council, is a reflection of this ongoing problem.
17. 'Le Concile, l'Église . . .', *art.cit.* (n. 1 above), p. 89.

Gaudium et Spes: the Forgotten Future of a Revolutionary Document

ERIC BORGMAN

Gaudium et spes, the Pastoral Constitution on the Church in the Modern World, is the epitome of the Second Vatican Council. The text, the first and so far the only example of a new genre of texts – a *constitutio pastoralis* was hitherto unheard of – was a sign of the spirit of renewal which John XXIII had called *aggiornamento*. One could say that *Gaudium et spes* was the Roman Catholic Church's first great effort to become genuinely modern. The Pastoral Constitution *Gaudium et spes* is modern insofar as it assumes that contemporary human beings live in a new era which cannot be understood by means of traditional ways of thinking and understanding. Not even traditional *religious and theological* ways of thinking and understanding. Modernity requires new, contemporary means of analysis and criteria of judgement.[1]

Even the very first section of the Constitution was a theological and religious revolution without comparison. This revolution made possible, first of all, important movements of renewal in the Church and in the theology of the last decades. This revolution was, second, the opening signal for fundamental theological controversies during these decades. It is however nevertheless more than ever of profound importance also for the future. However, the revolution of *Gaudium et spes* has during the last forty years been obviously neutralized by the mechanisms of the activities of the leadership of the Church. The document was put back into just that riverbed from which it had tried to break free: the tradition of Catholic Social Doctrine. There are however good arguments for the statement that the revolution of *Gaudium et spes* is still a revolution which the Church and theology are in need of. If and to what extent this revolution will in the future get the space it requires or is able to demand it, depends on a number of factors. However, reflection on what is at stake in terms of fundamental religious and theological concerns is in any case of great importance. Let us therefore begin by trying to describe the revolution signified by *Gaudium et spes*.

The revolution of profound interconnection

As we have already said, there is no precedence for a *'Pastoral Constitution for the Church in today's world'*. This led to an explanatory footnote being added to the title of the document which points out that the constitution is called 'pastoral' 'because, while resting on doctrinal principles, it seeks to express the relation of the Church to the world and modern mankind'. In its first part, the document develops the doctrine of the Church 'on man, on the world which is the enveloping context of man's existence, and on man's relations to his fellow men (sic!)'. In a second part it gives closer consideration to 'various aspects of modern life and human society; special consideration is given to those questions and problems which, in this general area, seem to have a greater urgency in our day', i.e. marriage and family, culture, socio-economic life, life in a political society and concern for peace. It is emphasized that the analysis of these questions is not merely concerned with their permanent elements but also with those which are transitory and that therefore the 'constitution must be interpreted according to the general norms of theological interpretation. Interpreters must bear in mind-especially in part two-the changeable circumstances which the subject matter, by its very nature, involves'.

Thus this footnote insinuates that what is new in *Gaudium et spes* is the fact that the document is explicitly concerned with contingent historical situations instead of seeking its orientation exclusively from the permanent doctrinal starting points. However, since in 1891 Leo XIII with his encyclical *Rerum novarum* founded the tradition of Catholic Social Doctrine, the Catholic Church has time and time again spoken on historical and social situations. According to the image held by the Catholic Church on its Social Doctrine this happens on the basis of principles which are taken to be permanent and entrusted to the Church by Jesus Christ. The footnote, inserted into *Gaudium et spes*, gives the impression that this constitution too takes this line, though with more extensive reflections on the current situation. The interpretation which under Pope John Paul II became increasingly the official interpretation, reflects this. Marie-Dominique Chenu showed in 1979 in an important study that the Social Doctrine of the Church was an ideology and that precisely in its emphasis on its permanence it was highly dependent in contemporary trains of social thinking.[2] It interpreted the 'signs of the times' and got involved with them with the help of contemporary methods of analysis and critique and in its polemic against them. *Gaudium et spes'* famous *adagium* that the Church was at all times called to test and interpret the signs of the times could thus be understood as an attempt to legitimize what had indeed frequently happened before. The official interpretation which had emerged during the pontificate of the late Pope seems to have revived the illusion already unmasked by Chenu that the Church is able to judge the world of today without effort on the basis of permanent principles.[3]

The approach of the Pastoral Constitution *Gaudium et spes* however meant a clear break with the Social Doctrine of the Church. This break was founded in a revolutionary shift in its ecclesiology and ultimately in fundamental theology as well as in the way in which it views the world theologically. Edward Schillebeeckx wrote shortly after the Council that the theological break-through of this way of thinking lay in its pastoral character. Schillebeeckx anticipated the actual danger the term 'pastoral', as used by Pope John XXIII from the beginning in connection with the Council, could be perceived as referring to the concrete application of doctrine of the faith which is fixed in itself.[4] It is however precisely this way of thinking which ceased to be in force with the Council. The Church as the messianic people of God was the light of the world. Thus Vatican II explained in its dogmatic constitution on the Church (LG II, 9). This could still be reconciled with the classic understanding of the Church as the guardian of an unchangeable revelation, which is God's gift to humanity, a revelation of which it takes care and responsibility. The pastoral constitution on the Church in the modern world however indicates clearly that the Church takes shape right at the heart of the world and comes into being. It does not first of all exist outside of the world as the guardian of God's revelation in order then to connect with the world, but it is formed right in the midst of the world. 'For theirs is a community composed of men. United in Christ, they are led by the Holy Spirit in their journey to the Kingdom of their Father . . .' (LG 1). As such, i.e. as living in the midst of the world and 'linked with mankind and its history by the deepest of bonds' the disciples who form the Church 'have welcomed the news of salvation which is meant for every man (sic!)'. Thus it is the task of the Church as the people of God and of the Council as its representative to proclaim 'the link of this people with the whole of humanity and the care and love of this people for the whole of humanity of which it is a part'. It is to enter into dialogue with humanity about the many and varied problems which it faces.

What matters is that in this way of thinking the world becomes the theological place for the disciples called by Christ to be his Church. Thus *Gaudium et spes* immediately follows the Dogmatic Constitution *Lumen gentium*. During the Council itself this was the subject of much argument and discussion. Hence the strong emphasis on the mere fact that in *Lumen gentium* the chapter about the People of God precedes that on the Church as hierarchy in the reception of *Lumen gentium*. To a certain extent it is even more remarkable how the Church is portrayed: 'the Church is in Christ like a sacrament or as a sign and instrument both of a very closely knit union with God and of the unity of the whole human race . . .' (LG 1). God is primarily called the creator and redeemer of the world who is recognized as such by the Church in a particular way and is present in it (LG 2-4). The Church does not exist for itself but it is a sign and an instrument of God's mission by which God takes humanity and the world into his own life. *Gaudium et spes* radicalizes this thought by explicitly qualifying the world in theological terms:

> Therefore, the council focuses its attention on the world of men, the whole human family along with the sum of those realities in the midst of which it lives; that world which is the theater of man's history, and the heir of his energies, his tragedies and his triumphs; that world which the Christian sees as created and sustained by its Maker's love, fallen indeed into the bondage of sin, yet emancipated now by Christ, Who was crucified and rose again to break the strangle hold of personified evil, so that the world might be fashioned anew according to God's design and reach its fulfillment. (GS 2, para 2)

'Présence au monde est présence à Dieu.', 'To be present in the world means to be present to God.' During the 1950s this was, borrowed from Dominique Lacordaire (1802–1861), the motto of the movement of the French Worker Priests. Twelve years before this movement had been stopped at Rome's instigation, due its perceived tendency to go too far in being concerned with the 'circumstances and concerns of the present day'.[5] Now by its approval of *Gaudium et spes* its starting point became officially the starting point of the Catholic Church.

A revolution half realized

In the reception of the Second Vatican Council the theological revolution, which *Gaudium et spes* represents was rarely acknowledged to its full extent. On a practical level the document's impact was great; this is certainly true for the time immediately after the Council. Together with *inter alia* Paul VI's Address on Peace before the General Assembly of the United Nations, together with the messages to those in government at the end of the Council, to intellectuals and scientists, to artists, to women, to workers, to the poor and to all who suffer, the Constitution bears witness to the fact that the

Catholic Church during the second half of the 1960s was a credible partner in the conversation about the world's problems.

In their efforts to formulate the results of the Council in a manner appropriate to their own social context the Conference of Latin American Bishops in 1968 organized a meeting in Medellín. On the basis of the words in *Gaudium et spes* that 'joys and the hopes, the griefs and the anxieties of the men of this age, especially those who are poor or in any way afflicted, these are the joys and hopes, the griefs and anxieties of the followers of Christ' (GS 1) they tried to understand what in their own context, shaped by poverty, oppression and violence would be the message of the Church embodied in world and deed. The document which was the result of this gathering marks the beginning of the theology of liberation which, in the words of Gustavo Gutiérrez, regards solidarity with the poor as a form of contemplation and of listening to God.[6] Thus the presence and the message of God were linked to the context of their own lives, and precisely in this the context of their own lives the presence and the message of God were truly to be found.[7]

Theologians outside of the Third World regarded the Theology of Liberation to a large extent as the expression of a political, social and social-ethical engagement and as its legitimization. Regardless of how much liberation theologians like Gutiérrez, Juan Luis Segundo, Jon Sobrino as well as Leonardo and Clodovis Boff tried to show the *theological* significance of liberation theology, most of their colleagues in the west continued to base its legitimacy on the classic theological method of working. As a consequence of this approach theological content, which had been traced through the analysis of the Bible and of the Church's tradition, was only subsequently linked with concrete situations. To this day this scheme is very influential. It goes without saying that one seeks to develop these analyses of the Bible, of the Tradition as well as of contemporary situations with the help of credible and up-to-date methodologies. The fundamental theological question implied by *Gaudium et spes* is often overlooked, let alone asked in a productive way: how can today's situation be analyzed theologically? How can theology, how can theologians hear the world where concrete human beings live into speech in a responsible way as the place where the footsteps of God are visible, footsteps of God as creator, redeemer and perfector and from there God's history with humankind?[8]

Nowadays theologians seem increasingly to turn away from this question, be it because it could become dangerous for orthodoxy, or because they think that it is impossible to answer it scientifically, and because today's academic culture puts them under pressure to focus on the study, the description and the explanation of religious practices.

Nevertheless precisely this question is obviously an important aspect of the forgotten future of the Second Vatican Council, which is the topic of this issue of *Concilium*.

In the footsteps of the incarnation

In 1985 theologians in South Africa published after wide ranging theological and ecclesial discussions and in the middle of the crisis in which the country found itself at the time, the so-called 'Kairos Document of South African Christians' as a theological commentary on the political situation. Two years later the white South African theologian Albert Nolan published a reflection on the way of doing theology which is necessary in order to produce such a document. In his text *God in South Africa* Nolan explicitly reversed the well-known idea that the content of the faith must remain the same across the changing times, but that formulations of the faith could and should change and be adapted to the times. According to Nolan it is the formulations of faith which must remain the same: it should always be the good news which has given hope to human beings in their concrete situations, hope for liberation from that which held them captive and oppressed them. The content of the faith should have to adapt to that. Nolan uses a number of biblical examples to show that the history of faith is held together not by one and the same conviction with regard to content. Rather in concrete situations there has been time and time again hopeful orientation towards liberation from suffering, oppression and hopelessness.[9]

Like for example that of Gustavo Gutiérrez, Nolan's approach goes back to the work of the French theologian and Dominican Marie-Dominique Chenu. *Une école de théologie: Le Saulchoir* It is characteristic of the strange progress of the history of Catholic theology during the twentieth century that this important and reviving book remained out of print for more than fifty years. In 1937 Chenu reproduced the text as a typescript the distribution of which remained extremely limited. In 1942 the book and its author were condemned, and its proper publication did not take place until 1985.[10] What makes this book important in terms of theology and thus the subject of ecclesial debate is the approach to theology which Chenu develops here. For him theology was ultimately reflection on the human situation of today and on the way in which God himself is affected by it. According to Chenu himself, this was his interpretation of Thomas Aquinas' view that faith experiences life and theology studies the world *sub ratione Dei*, in relation to God. In addition to being a theologian, Chenu was also a historian, and he showed that the great theological visions of the past were not systems enclosed within themselves. They were forms reflection on the contemporary situation out of a specific spirituality and in the context of a very specific culture. God's revelation cannot just be found in the Bible and the Church's Tradition, but in the faith of human beings which moves beyond it and reacts to new situations time and time again and in the intellectual reflection towards it, theology. These together constitute the Tradition. Furthermore, according to Chenu, those things which are done here and now out of faith and proclaimed theologically, can only be discovered through recognizing and interpreting the signs of the times in the light of the gospel. In his view, the Church is to take on its liberating incarnation again and again throughout history.[11]

Chenu's view forms the background of the approach of *Gaudium et spes*. This view however vividly asks the question about the identity of faith and the Church. If however the Christian message cannot be defined in terms of its substance, but is as it were required to develop afresh again and again in responding to the signs of the times, what then is the foundation of the continuity of this faith? The Pastoral Constitution *Gaudium et spes* avoids this question by giving the impression of merely applying the permanent doctrine of the Church to the present situation. Chenu and Nolan, but ultimately also Schillebeeckx, place God's liberating presence in creation. From its beginning the world has been created by God with a view to salvation and liberation, and Jesus brings this aim and destination of creation to light.[12] The Church's task is to walk in the footsteps of Jesus and to do the same. This ultimately leads Schillebeeckx to the conclusion that what is normative, from the perspective of faith, are not Jesus' words and actions but the relationship between the words and the deeds of Jesus on the one hand and their context on the other. Believers here and now are not asked to imitate what Jesus said or did, rather they are to relate to their context as Jesus related to his. According to Schillebeeckx, what matters is not the same, but the same in proportion, the same in relation.[13] This could however suggest that the Church requires again and again a repetition of the incarnation, to take on flesh in varying contexts of human history where 'the mind that was in Jesus Christ' (Phil. 2.5) comes to life. The thought that God would have to take the initiative again and again for the faith to become an adequate answer to a particular situation, undermines however the uniqueness of the incarnation of God in Jesus Christ and its abiding value for the history that follows him. The idea that each time anew a creative initiative on the part of human beings is required which form the Church in a particular place and in a particular time, obscures the insight that from a Christian perspective faith is always a response to God's initiative.

Theological epistemology: an open question

Thus we have arrived at what is in my view the real 'forgotten future' of *Gaudium et spes*. This is the question of today's theological epistemology: what does it mean to interpret the signs of the times 'in the light of the Gospel'? And what is in this context the role of these signs and what the role of the gospel? It is impossible to answer these questions in the few remaining lines of this article. They require yet further profound reflection and study. It should however be clear that in any case there must be signs that can be interpreted. This means that God's presence in his creation and God's incarnation amidst the ambiguities of human history precedes faith and theology. God's saving presence must, theologically speaking, be a given and cannot be the product of theological theory or the project of faith. The same applies to the dynamics of the world in its orientation to the kingdom of God; theology only makes sense, if the kingdom of God as Jesus proclaimed it is indeed at hand. At the same time we need the 'light of the gospel', in order to be able to see the signs of the times indeed as signs of God's saving presence and in order to be able to make them visible as such to others. Without the light which shines through the witness of living crucified that which, in Christian terms, is a sign of God's impending salvation amidst suffering and death merely as *one* of the many random adversities of human fate to which our existence is subject by its very nature. Where human beings begin from within the Church and as Church to make visible the signs of the times as signs of the impending kingdom of God, there the Church appears indeed 'like a sacrament or as a sign and instrument both of a very closely knit union with God and of the unity of the whole human race' (LG, 1).

Amidst all the pressures which are put on to theology to become the study of religion, it has to hold on to the fact that the contribution it makes to the Church is an indispensable part of its task. Theology is neither the servant of the Church not does it serve society's desire to obtain greater knowledge and greater access to religion. In the end of the day, theology is in the service of God who according to Christian conviction is liberator and redeemer and as such at the same time always already also creator. Regardless of how much the world appears to misunderstand this, ultimately its being comes from the God who desires for human beings to have life in abundance and who gives it to them. The most prominent theological task is the reflection as to *how* this paradox can be thought in a credible way.

Translated by Natalie K. Watson

Notes

1. For this understanding of modernity cf. Michel Foucault, 'Qu'est-ce que les Lumières?' in M. Foucault, *Dits et écrits*, Paris, 1994, 562–578; here: 568–570.
2. Marie-Dominique Chenu, *La doctrine sociale de l'Église comme idéologie*, Paris, 1979.
3. The return to the Social Doctrine of the Church already began with Paul VI's Apostolic Letter *Octogesima adveniens* (14 May 1971) and was completed with the encyclicals of John Paul II: *Laborem exercens* (14 September 1981), *Sollicitudo rei socialis* (30 December 1981) und *Centesimus annus* (1 May 1991). The instruction of the Congregation for the Doctrine of the Faith *Libertatis conscientia* (22 March 1986) explicitly presents the Social Doctrine of the Church as an alternative to the theology of liberation. Liberation theology however is, as we will see more clearly later on, in its origin dependent on the impulse of *Gaudium et spes*.
4. Edward Schillebeeckx, *Het tweede Vaticaans concilie* II, Tielt/Den Haag, 1966.
5. For the conflict regarding worker priests cf. L. Leprieur, *Quand Rome condamne: Dominicains et prêtres-ouvriers*, Paris, 1989. The words cited which are meant pejoratively are from Pius XII's encyclical *Humani generis* (12 August 1959), 11f.
6. Cf. E.L. Cleary, *Crisis and Change: The Church in Latin America Today*, Maryknoll 1985; cf. especially chapter 2. This can be found on the internet at http://www.dominicans.org/ecleary/crisis/.
7. This can already be found in Gustavo Gutiérrez' *A Theology of Liberation* (SCM 1972), but it is even more clearly developed in his later books *The Power of the Poor in History* (Maryknoll 1983) and *We Drink from Our Own Wells: Spiritual Journey of a People*, (Maryknoll 1984 (1983)).
8. Cf my book *Sporen van de bevrijdende God* (Kampen, 1990). In my article 'Theology as the Art of Liberation: Edward Schillebeeckx's Response to the Theologies of the EATWOT' (*Exchange* 32 (2003), 98–108) I show that Schillebeeckx is an important exception among western academic theologians.
9. Albert Nolan, *God in South Africa: The Challenge of the Gospel*, Capetown and Johannesburg, 1987.
10. Marie-Dominique Chenu, *Une école de théologie: Le Saulchoir*, Paris 1985.
11. Cf Ch. F. Potworowski, *Contemplation and Incarnation: The Theology of Marie-Dominque Chenu*, Montréal/Kingston, 2001, pp. 156–163. Cf also: Marie-Dominique Chenu, *La Parole de Dieu*, Paris, 1964 and *Peuple de Dieu dans le monde*, Paris, 1966.
12. Cf primarily E. Schillebeeckx, *Tussentijds verhaal over twee Jezusboeken*, Bloemendaal, 1978, pp. 121–140: 'Rijk van God: Schepping en heil' (The Kingdom of God: Creation and Salvation').
13. Cf primarily Schillebeckx' final speech as a professor: 'Theologisch geloofsverstaan anno 1983' Baarn 1989; part of this was later published in: *Mensen als verhaal van God*, Baarn 1989. Schillebeeckx borrows this thought from Clodovis Boff, *Teologia e prática: Teologia do politico e suas mediaçoes*, Petrópolis, 1979.

Forty Years Later: What has become of the Ecclesiological Reforms envisaged by Vatican II?

HERVÉ LEGRAND

It would require a historical or even multi-disciplinary approach to do justice to the ecclesiastical reforms brought in by Vatican II. Here I am providing simply a theological reading of them, with reference to the aim proposed for the Council by John XXIII. With remarkable insight, he had linked pastoral reform to ecumenical outreach.[1] Announcing a diocesan synod for Rome and a general reform of canon law together meant that *aggiornamento* depended on a renewal of diocesan churches and of the figure of the Catholic bishop,[2] linked to a major reform of institutions, which the Council would prepare.

This agenda became that of the bishops. In general terms, the 'papal monarchy' identified with the dogmas of Vatican I presented a pastoral and missionary handicap,[3] not to say an ecumenical stumbling-block.[4] The bishops' sustained sympathy for the 'Secretariat for Unity' confirmed this perceived link between ecumenism and reforms. Their support for episcopal collegiality, seen as the necessary counterweight to Vatican I, was to crystallize this sympathy. John XXIII's intuition was therefore perfectly understood in this respect; what is less clear is whether it was as well understood in relation to institutional reforms.

Vatican II paid scant attention to the canonical dimension of the reforms it sought to introduce. Of all the Council documents, only the Constitution on the Liturgy concerned itself with guaranteeing its enactment, setting out forty-nine (!) normative prescriptions. After this, *Christus Dominus* was virtually the only document to use this method, though it set out wishes rather than norms.[5] This was to be the method of Vatican II as a whole, and it did not devote a single plenary session to reform of the Code of Canon Law. It severely criticized the Curia, but without issuing any directives to reform it. Its vocabulary, with 1135 mentions of 'Church' and only five of 'canon law',[6] clearly shows that it refrained from drawing up a law to accord with its ecclesiology. Was this due only to the fact that the canon law of the time, cut off from its rich history, presented no more than a cramped vision of ecclesiology to the majority interested in various forms of renewal and therefore suspicious of canon law?[7] That is a question for historians to answer.

The treatment of episcopal collegiality, the central plank of Vatican II's institutional reform, favoured theological discourse, to the detriment of law. The majority placed their confidence in the theologians. These saw the vote approving collegiality as 'the dorsal fin of the whole Council', 'the centre of gravity of Vatican II'.[8] The future cardinal Yves Congar even wrote that with this vote, 'We came to feel that it had been done. Vatican II had redressed the balanced of Vatican I [. . .] by a majority that never fell below 87%'.[9]

According to Congar, Vatican II had thereby achieved its aim: 'To give the episcopate back a more important and initiating role in the actual governance of the Church, at present dominated by a manner of exercising papal primacy, a manner bearing the stamp of the Curia and Roman centralization,[10] [which presents] a stumbling-block to all the other Churches, which view papal power as absolutist and monarchical.'[11] As a historian of institutions, by the following year he saw the need to nuance this general optimism: 'Only the future and practice will tell what this doctrine of collegiality will bring both to possibilities for ecumenical dialogue and to the balance between papal and episcopal functions within the Catholic Church. They will also tell whether a beginning of a theology of local Churches, contained in *Lumen Gentium* and taken up in *Ad Gentes*, will have found an echo in the life of the Church, and with what ecumenical impact.'[12]

Forty years later, do we have answers to these questions? What has become of *collegiality*, the expression of the will of the bishops to be the controllers of the general orientations of the Church? What is now the status of the *episcopal conferences* that were destined to allow a partnership among the diocesan Churches, in their regions and even in the whole Church? Finally, did the *reform of canon law*, or that of the Curia, correspond to the wishes of Vatican II? The answers are spread over two periods, that of the pontificate of Paul VI, then that of John Paul II.

I. The first reception of Vatican II: a revaluation of the episcopate and of local Churches, faithful to the letter of Vatican II

During the Council itself

Paul VI, aware of the mood of the bishops, took the initiative in revaluing their status. Starting in November 1963, he 'conceded' them a series of 'faculties', partially freeing them from their stunning degree of dependence on the Roman Curia.[13] Still *motu proprio*, Paul VI channelled the wish of the episcopate to participate ordinarily in defining the main lines of the life of the Church, by instituting a synod of bishops to work with him,[14] 'directly and immediately subject to Our authority', which would be master neither of its composition nor of its order of the day (n. III), and which would have only 'a temporary and occasional authority' (n. I).

When Paul VI undertook the implementation of the Council,[15] all his reforms were to be marked by the same spirit. The conciliar requests would be honoured, in the sense that local Churches began to be upgraded around their bishop, as was the episcopate in relation to the Holy See, but within the unchanged framework of a 'pontifical monarchy' conceived as inseparable from the dogmas of Vatican I.[16]

A revaluation of dioceses around their bishop

Ecclesiae Sanctae (1966) was an important reform. It gave bishops new institutional partners at the heart of their Church: councils of priests (n. 15) and pastoral councils (n. 16). It took the first steps in renewing relations with Religious (nn. 22–40). It introduced a closer correlation between the bishop and his Church, by better integrating the figure of coadjutor and auxiliary (nn. 13–14) and introducing an age limit for tenure of office (n. 11). Finally, it defined the status of episcopal conferences (n. 41). Nevertheless, the bishop continued to hold all powers in his hands. The chapter of *Lumen Gentium* (ch. II) on the people of God might not have been written, as shown by the silence on diocesan synods.

A revaluation of the episcopate in relation to the Holy See

De episcoporum muneribus (1966), in conformity with the norms laid down in *Christus Dominus* 8, replaces the regime of concession of powers to the bishops by the pope with that of papal reserve. On the level of principle, this is a major pastoral and ecumenical reform. The bishops henceforward have, in their diocese, all the powers 'required for the exercise of their pastoral office', with the pope 'reserving [only some] cases to himself' for the sake of the good of the whole Church. But in practice the adoption of this norm had hardly any effect.

Beyond the diocese, the episcopate was enhanced by the creation or the confirmation of a number of institutions. Episcopal conferences, which were made obligatory where they were not already in existence, were granted only a modest role of coordinating pastoral work. They could choose their delegates to the synod held with the pope. Furthermore, in accordance with *Christus Dominus* 38, 5, conferences could be formed from many nations on a continent, on the model of CELAM. Enjoying consultative power, they could strengthen awareness of regional Churches. This would promote a degree of diversity in unity, as the Patriarchates of the early Church had done,[17] which would prevent confusion between Catholicism and universalism.

In 1967 *Pro comperto sane* laid down that seven diocesan bishops, without residing in Rome, would normally form part of the *Plenaria* of each dicastery. Also in 1967, through the same *motu proprio* and a new arrangement of the Roman Curia, this was partially internationalized and was to receive a new structure with the official accreditation of new Secretariats, particularly those for Christian Unity, Inter-religious Dialogue, and Justice and Peace. While the Curia was thus given new tasks and brought more into contact with the realities of local Churches, nothing in its ecclesiological status was changed.

Pope Paul VI's reforms: an extensive rearrangement of a framework inherited from Vatican I

With great intellectual care and respect for persons, Paul VI thus carried out considerably far-reaching reforms, making consultative structures a general principle. But because these reforms did not constitute local and regional Churches as legal bodies capable of taking initiatives as part of the Church as a whole, their ecumenical and pastoral effect was modest. In practice they re-introduced monarchical regimes at every level – parish, diocese, whole Church[18] – tempered, it is true, with consultation, but pretty far from the requests for participation, decentralization, and collegiality that had been indicators of a new Christian social awareness at Vatican II. Rendered rather inefficient by this distance, these monarchical regimes were also perceived as 'culturally arbitrary' in the Weberian sense of the term.

They were arbitrary because the absolute power of the 'hierarchy'[19] appeared to plagiarize certain secular values of European societies between 1850 and 1950, a period when the Church, like the monarchical State, experienced a first modernization, of a legal and bureaucratic nature, characterized by processes of rationalization, centralization, and greater uniformity.[20] In societies that were still rural, deeply hierarchical, little educated, slower to change than they are today and then changing from the top down, the papal magisterium from Leo XIII to Pius XII consistently developed an ecclesiology that set apart 'governors and governed', 'teachers and taught', 'priests and helpers', upholding a cultural ethos in which the principal values were obedience to authority, collective discipline, and durability of rites and doctrines, all of which went in tandem with rejection of innovations.

In an urbanized, educated, technically complex, rapidly changing, and on principle egalitarian society, on the other hand, this earlier ethos seemed to make arbitrary selections of Christian values. Furthermore, it proved unworkable when innovation, participation, initiative, partnership and group discussion, negotiated rather than bestowed reforms are the order of the day, while ongoing changes no longer allow for literal repetition of tradition and require that it be interpreted.

Through its basic decision to place the chapter on the people of God before that on the hierarchy (LG chs. II and III), and through its requests for synodality and collegiality, for a structured linkage of the responsibilities of 'all', of 'some', and of 'one only', Vatican II had found a means of fruitful engagement with this new cultural situation, without ever drifting into democracy. In the event, the conceptual choices made in canon law reform, which John XXII had seen to be essential, served only to confirm the universally valid legal models once again favoured during the latter part of the papacy of John Paul II.

II. The second reception of Vatican II: accentuation of the prerogatives of the universal Church at the expense of the local Church and the episcopate

In John XXIII's plan, the Code of Canon Law needed to be reformed in order put the Council's *aggiornamento* into effect. In fact, through its arrangement and its vocabulary, as through its confirmation of the close dependence of the bishops on the pope, the 1983 Code, and even its 1990 revision, is far removed from the pastoral and ecumenical outlook the Council Fathers had wished to develop under the name of collegiality.[21]

The arrangement of the 1983 Code ignores the revaluation of local Churches and impedes understanding of the Church as communion of Churches.

In its Book II, materially faithful to *Lumen Gentium*, which begins with the people of God, the Code deals, in Part I, with the status of the faithful, clergy and laity, and, in Part II, section 1, with supreme power in the Church and the college of bishops. So it is *after* considering bishops that it turns to their dioceses, which it systematically refers to as 'particular Churches' (Part II, section 2). The Code therefore establishes in terms of ecclesiology what lay people and clerics are, what a pope and the college of bishops, the synod of bishops, the college of cardinals, the Roman Curia and papal nuncios are, before even establishing what a local Church is! Such a procedural choice prevents a vision of the Church as a communion of Churches and therefore entails, as we shall see, the disassociation of the communion of bishops from the communion of Churches,[22] thereby logically generating pastoral and ecumenical obstacles in a single process.

Unlike Vatican II, which saw the diocese as a portion of the Church, the Code tended to make it a part of the universal Church.

The choice of the neologism 'particular Church' to designate dioceses technically and systematically had a considerable ecclesiological impact, since Vatican II saw them as *portions* (see, e.g., LG 23b), refusing to see them as *parts*, which would not contain the true essence of the Church in themselves. The choice of a word deriving from the root *pars* to describe them runs the risk of inferring a theologically deficient understanding of the relationship between dioceses and the whole Church. In Latin, in the Romance languages, in German, and in English, 'particular' is lexicographically the antonym of 'universal'. Even involuntarily, such a choice is pregnant with a pure and simple subordination of the 'particular Churches' to the universal Church. Recognizing them as 'portions' would have placed them as partners with full rights in the Church, which was the clear wish of Vatican II.

The revised Code stresses the authority of the Holy See over bishops and over each bishop.

According to the teaching of LG 27, bishops are 'vicars and ambassadors of Christ' and should not 'be regarded as vicars of the Roman Pontiff'. The Code is silent on the title of vicar for bishops and reserves it to the pope, 'Head of the college of bishops, Vicar of Christ and Pastor of the whole

Church' (can. 331). As for bishops: 'Against a sentence or a decree of the Roman Pontiff, there is no appeal or recourse' (can. 333, 3); likewise, 'It falls to the Roman Pontiff, in accordance with the needs of the Church, to choose and to promote the forms in which the college of bishops will collegially carry out their task in relation to the whole Church' (can. 337, 3). The terms of their *Oath of Fidelity* since 1987[23] and those of the new Code give bishops a status in relation to the pope that canonists equate with that of a vicar general in relation to his bishop.[24] Is that being faithful to the letter of Vatican II?

The Code of Canons of the Eastern Churches since 1990

Despite establishing the concept of Churches *sui iuris*, this Code makes their administration increasingly uniform. It amalgamates the somewhat heterogeneous canonical traditions of the Churches of Byzantium and Ethiopia, or those of Armenia and Syriac India, and it does so in Latin, despite Eastern anxieties over Latinization.[25] Finally, the Pope promulgated it on his own, without associating the Heads of these Churches with it,[26] and some of its provisions widen his primatial power still further.[27] Nevertheless, the status of diocesan bishop is better safeguarded in this Code than in that of the Latin Church.

The reform of the Curia has confirmed its prerogatives as instrument of the primacy.

Given a rough ride at the Council, the Curia has since experienced unparalleled growth. The new Code confirms it as the pope's instrument in the 'daily' governance of the Church,[29] as does *Pastor Bonus* (1988), which is its latest reform. Its staff has more than doubled, while the number of bishops in it has quadrupled, from around twenty in the time of Pius XII to more than eighty today, a sort of permanent synod. . . . The numbers on its staff roughly equate to the number of diocesan bishops.[30] Furthermore, the different dicasteries often have their documents approved by the pope in specific form, providing their own theology and history, while papal teaching has never been so provided.[31] There has been only a rudimentary start to implementing the wishes of the Council Fathers to see the principle of subsidiarity extended.[33]

Between 1992 and 2000, the Curia has fully regained its central place.

There is no space here to analyze the decisions that sent both bishops and theologians, who had, as a body, played the leading roles at Vatican II, back to their usual places. So, leaving the fate of theologians to one side,[34] I shall limit myself to more structural developments.

1. *Limitation of the expression of diocesan synods (1997).* The 'Instruction on Diocesan Synods', issued jointly by the Congregations for Bishops and for the Evangelization of Peoples, forbids them to formulate a simple 'wish to transmit to the Holy See' if this diverges 'from theses or positions [held by] the permanent teaching of the Church or the Pontifical magisterium or concerns disciplinary matters reserved to the higher ecclesiastical authority or to another'. Local Churches are thus subjects at law only within very narrow limits. Even in the disciplinary sphere, where many matters are left to them, they have to cultivate conformity to the 'universal Church'.[35]

2. *Reduction of the modest standing of bishops' conferences (Apostolos suos and Ad tuendam Fidem* (1997). *Lumen Gentium* 23 expected bishops' conferences to express a legitimate pluriformity within the Church, on the model of the ancient Patriarchates, an expectation that their original, over-modest, canonical status did not allow them to fulfil. In *Apostolos suos,* their very existence is made dependent on the act of the Holy See that institutes them and decides their powers (nn. 13 and 20).[36] It takes away the authentic magisterium they exercised under canon 753 of the Latin Code, except when their decision is unanimous.[37] The bishops 'gathered in the episcopal conference' are expected to 'take care above all to follow the magisterium of the universal Church and to make it known opportunely to the people entrusted to them' (n. 21). In short, to be handers-on of the teaching of the Holy See,[38] which retains strict control of the interpretation of the Christian faith in all cultures throughout the entire world.

3. *Discouragement of the possibility of understanding the Catholic Church as a communion of Churches (Communionis notio,* 1992). Faithful to patristic theology, LG 23 declared that 'In and from such individual churches there comes into being the one and only Catholic Church', which allows it to be viewed as a communion of Churches, a proposal full of pastoral and ecumenical interest. The Curia[39] rejected this interpretation, in practice and in theory. The first expression of this is expressed in *Communionis notio*: 'The universal Church is an ontologically and chronologically previous reality to any single particular Church.' Such a proposition is certainly true in the sense that no Church can call itself Catholic outside the communion of the whole Church, outside the network of *traditio-receptio* that forms the

Catholica through time and space. But the continuation of the text is less convincing: 'Ontologically [...] the Church, one and only, according to the Fathers, precedes the creation of and gives birth to the particular Churches as to her own daughters; she is expressed in them; she is mother and not product of the particular Churches [...]. Demonstrating her universality since its origin, she has given birth to the different local Churches as particular embodiments of the one and only Church. As they are born in the Church and from the universal Church, it is from her and in her that they have their ecclesiality. Consequently, the formula of Vatican II: the Church "in and from [such individual] churches" (*ecclesia in et ex ecclesiis*, LG 23) is inseparable from this other formula: the Churches in and from the Church (*ecclesiae in et ex ecclesia*)' (CN 9).

Repeated in *Apostolos suos* (1997) and the 'Secret Letter' of the Congregation for the Doctrine of the Faith (2000), this reasoning presents certain difficulties:

First difficulty: Does the ontological priority of the universal Church over 'any singular particular Church' imply its priority over *all* the particular Churches? This would oblige us to imagine that the universal Church could exist *prior* to the actual confessional and sacramental processes that institute it and *independently* of these same processes, so apart from its believers and the sacraments of the faith. Such a Church would be 'a creation of reason',[40] which nothing obliges us to postulate, not even the pre-existence of the Church in God's plan, which could include the simultaneity of Church and Churches. The same concept leads to the addition that, 'the episcopal college is a reality pre-dating the office of being head of a particular Church' (*ibid.*), with the many bishops without dioceses adduced as proof.[41]

Second difficulty: The 'motherhood of the universal Church with regard to particular Churches' would be the foundation for this priority. The motherhood of the Church with regard to the faith of the faithful is well attested in tradition,[42] as is the motherhood of a founding Church with regard to one it has founded. On the other hand, the idea of the motherhood of the universal Church with regard to all local Churches never seems to have been formulated.[43]

Third difficulty: This discourse of universal motherhood, coupled with that of an exclusive identification of the Catholic Church with the universal Church, abandons (as does the 'Secret Letter')[44] the ecclesiological tradition we have in common with the Orthodox Church.[45] Notably, by declaring that the successor of Peter '*already belongs to the essence of every particular Church "from within"*' (CN 13), are we not risking turning the Bishop of Rome into a sort of universal bishop?

These difficulties taken together probably explain the general reticence of the theological community toward these doctrinal developments.[46] Specifically, they also justify that of Cardinal Kasper, who fears a confusion between the motherhood of the universal Church and that of the Church of Rome: 'The formulation becomes altogether problematic if the one universal Church is surreptitiously [*unter den Hand*] identified with the Church of Rome – *de facto* with the pope and the Curia. If this were the case, then the Letter from the Congregation for the Doctrine of the Faith could not be understood as an *aide-mémoire* to clarifying the ecclesiology of communion, but would have to be understood as its abandonment [*Verabschiedung*] and as an attempt at theological restoration of Roman centralization.'[47]

Conclusion

One observation can bring this summary account to a conclusion: since the peaceful public exchanges between Cardinals Kasper and Ratzinger,[48] it seems that no new element has been added from one side or the other. What can one then conclude about the fate of the reforms emanating from Vatican II?

The breadth of reforms carried out needs to be stressed: the liturgy and the word of God are accessible to all; ecumenism is here to stay; interfaith dialogue is accepted (thanks to John Paul II); a process of consultation has been generalized; mindsets have been extensively changed, as has the public image of the Church.

But one major question is still to be answered: Have the reforms of Vatican II achieved their first objective: to correct the unwanted effects of Vatican I? It is more pertinent to ask this than to embark on a quarrel over the letter and the spirit of the Council. The fact is that when collegiality has been interpreted in a more 'affective than effective' fashion, the head being able to do everything without the college, and the latter being able to do nothing without the head; when all the authority given to priests, bishops, and pope remains consultative; when the communion of Churches has been subsumed into the communion of the Church, one can well ask whether the intentions (which are not the 'spirit') of Vatican II have been effectively honoured. The reforms brought in have not been able to overcome the persistent pastoral and ecumenical obstacles.

On the pastoral level, the reforms were proposed as universally valid, and so obliged to be of the 'legal-bureaucratic' type; they are rarely adapted locally to the millions of faithful living in the most diverse cultures. Such a system has not allowed the pope – John Paul II's travels had a different aim

– or the Curia to concentrate, with their due authority, on the Churches to help bring about solutions that they themselves alone can work out. The system put in place has centred the Churches on the Roman Curia, which legislates, sometimes down to the last detail, and controls in a universal manner, at the risk of thereby removing responsibility from the local players. This gives rise to recurrent problems relating to models of authority, the choice of bishops, the varying status of women, or recruitment of the clergy.[49] Universal collegiality will be no better able to resolve these questions than the Curia. The creation of continent-wide conferences would provide some elements of a solution,[50] provided a climate of confidence and patience were generated.[51]

On the ecumenical level, an evolution in this direction would, over the long term and provided other factors come together, create good conditions for the reunion of Christians, as the unitary Church has been shown to be historically opposed to the one Church.[52] On the ecumenical level, as on the pastoral level, the priorities are the same: to work for a theological and epistemological renewal of canon law and above all to re-assess the hermeneutics of Vatican I, even before those of Vatican II.

Translated by Paul Burns

Notes

1. *Osservatore Romano*, 26–7 Jan. 1959: 'The Council does not envisage only the good of the Christian people [. . .] it also seeks to be an invitation to separated communities to search for Unity.'
2. Angelo Roncalli's work on Charles Borromeo had prepared him to think in this way.
3. The powers conceded by *Pastorali munus* (Nov. 1963) leave no doubt on this point.
4. Paul VI himself was to say that the pope is 'the most serious obstacle on the road to ecumenism': *Allocution to the Secretariat for Unity*, 1967. In *Ut unum sint*, John Paul II asked for the help of other Christians on this point.
5. The decree ends by referring their working out to the future Code, having introduced no restrictive rules itself except in its no. 8. The other decrees are content with wishes (PO 20 and AG 16, 29).
6. LG 45, AG 19, CD 44, AA 1.
7. Could Bishop De Smedt's popular denunciation of 'triumphalism, clericalism, and legalism' in one go have indicated a confusion, in the atmosphere of the time, between legalism and rights?
8. Without citing his sources, Card. Eyt attributed the first proposition to U. Betti

and the second to A. Wenger: 'La collégialité épiscopale', in *Le deuxième concile du Vatican*, Rome 1989, p. 54.
9. Yves Congar, *Le concile au jour le jour. Troisième session*, Paris 1964, p. 44.
10. *Ibid.*, p. 37.
11. *Idem, Le concile au jour le jour*, Paris 1963, p. 18.
12. *Idem., Le concile ... Quatrième session*, Paris 1966, p. 134.
13. *Motu proprio Pastorale munus*, AAS 56, 1964, 5–12. To save space I shall henceforth give documents their Latin title alone, without reference to AAS. These can be found in my more detailed 'Les évêques, les Eglises locales et l'Eglise entière', *Revue des sciences philosophiques et théologiques* 85 (2001), 461–509; 'La théologie des Eglises soeurs. Réflexions ecclésiologiques autour de la Déclaration de Balamand', ibid. 88 (2004), 461–96.
15. In Jan. 1966 the *Motu proprio finis concilio* created the Post-conciliar Central Commission, which was not a continuation committee mandated by the Council Fathers: the implementation of the Council, and its interpretation, reverted to the pope.
16. Congar anticipated this possibility: Vatican II 'so often affirms the pontifical primacy and the dogma of Vatican I that it is quite possible that for an initial period it will harden rather than dissipate opposition from the Orthodox': *Le concile ..., op. cit.* 1963, p. 47. A. Acerbi comments: 'Recognition of the authority of bishops over the universal Church is not translated [in the Code] into any legal formulation that would operate apart from papal authority.' This remains 'absolute' or 'purely monarchical, as one prefers': 'Per una nuova forma del ministero petrino' in A. Acerbi (ed.), *Il ministero del papa in prospettiva ecumenica*, Milan 1999, p. 308.
17. LG 23 expresses a wish in this regard.
18. A proposal by Card. Schotte, secretary general of the synod of bishops, though journalistic, is still revealing: 'The bishops are accountable to no one, except to the pope. And the pope is accountable to no one except Jesus.' *The Tablet*, 17 Nov. 2001, p. 1630.
19. The term is used in its technical sense of 'political regime in which the holder of power attached to his person, concentrating all powers in his hands, governs without any control', according to the definition by H. Morel, *Dictionnaire de philosophie politique*, ed. P. Raynaud and S. Rials, Paris 1996, p. 1.
20. The victory of ultramontanism at Vatican I, the first-ever codification of canon law in 1917, the uniformity imposed on liturgy (suppression of Gallican rites), on theology (the spread of 'Denziger', the suppression of modernism), on morals (diffusion of manuals for confessors), on the clergy (generalization of minor and major seminaries, continued wearing of uniform), and so on make up a revealing series of parallels.
21. I use this term, though it is lacking in Vatican II, to encapsulate the plan of the majority.
22. W. F. Rothe has lucidly described this arrangement: 'It implies the priority of

the concept of particular Church over that of diocesan Church, of the episcopate of apostolic succession over the diocesan episcopate, and finally that of the universal Church over the particular Church': 'Kanonistische Anmerkungen zum Verhältnis von Universalkirche und Partikularkirche', *Forum Katholische Theologie* 18 (2002), 224–32.

23. Where it states: 'I swear to remain always faithful to the Catholic Church and to (N) its supreme pastor, to the vicar of Jesus Christ and to the successor of Peter in the primacy as well as at the head of the college of bishops [. . .]. I will obey the free exercise of the primatial power of the pope over the whole Church; I will endeavour to promote and to defend his rights and his authority. I will accept and respect the prerogatives and the exercise of ministry of the papal envoys, who represent him [. . .]. I will account for my pastoral mandate to the Apostolic See at dates fixed in advance or on specified occasions, and it most willingly that I will accept their orders or their counsels and will zealously put them into operation.'

24. This is the conclusion G. Bier comes to in his doctoral thesis, *Die Rechtsstellung des Diözesanbischofs nach den Codex Iuris Canonici von 1983*, Würzburg 2001, p. 376. Canon 480 provides that, 'The vicar general and the vicar apostolic should account to the diocesan bishop on the main matters in hand and those already dealt with, and they shall never act against the wish or the desire of the diocesan bishop'.

25. A fear that was far from baseless: see the (unexecuted) decree of 4 Mar. 1998, deciding to expel all legitimately married Greek Catholic priests working in Poland to Ukraine and to replace them with celibate bi-ritual Latin priests. Text in *Istina* 44 (1999), 278–89.

26. The papal formula of approval of the Acts of Vatican II could have served as a precedent: cf. G. Alberigo, 'Una cum patribus. La formule conclusive des decisions de Vatican II' in *Ecclesia a Spiritu Sancto edocta*, 1970, pp. 291–319.

27. Acording to canon 412 of the CCEO, copied from the Latin Code, 'all religious are subject to the Supreme Pontiff, as to their supreme superior, whom they are bound to obey by reason of their vow of obedience'. Furthermore, according to canon 1008, 1: 'The Roman Pontiff is the supreme administrator and dispenser of all the temporal goods of the Church', which is clarified in sec. 2: 'As to the right of ownership of the temporal goods of the Church, it is under the authority of the Roman Pontiff that this belongs to the juridical person who has legitimately acquired them'. The fixing of an upper limit for the alienation of a good might have avoided an expression that would be misunderstood in Orthodox monasticism.

28. Cf H. Legrand, 'L'évêque éparchial. Quelques évaluations ecclésiologiques et oecuméniques des options systématiques du *CCEO*' in *Ius vehiculum caritatis*, Vatican City 2004, 117–44.

29. This *cura cotidiana* is deduced from canon 249.

30. Figures derived from research into the 60, then 156, pages devoted to the

Roman Curia in the *Annuario Pontifico* of 1954 and 2004. For around 2,500 dioceses, there are now some 2,400 curial members.

31. Thus the *Instructio* issued by eight dicasteries on the collaboration of lay faithful in the ministry of priests (1997) firmly states 'the theologically certain doctrine and age-old practice of the Church according to which the only valid minister [of the anointing of the sick] is the priest' (art. 9, 2). According to A. Chavasse, *Étude sur l'onction des infirmes dans l'Église latine du 3e siècle à l réforme carolingienne*, Lyon 1942, the anointing was often done by a family member, using oil blessed by the bishop.
32. Its *Insegnamenti* each year run to between 4,000 (1982) and 5,000 (1988) pages.
33. One example: when the matter could have been left to the discretion of parish priests, advised where necessary by their vicar general, in 1992 the Pontifical Council for the Interpretation of Legislative Texts, faced with a *dubium* on the possibility of young girls serving Mass, replied in the affirmative on principle, 'according to instructions to come from the Holy See'. Four conditions are detailed in AAS 86 (1994), 541–2.
34. The creation of the International Theological Commission in 1969 did not have all the effects expected of it, since *Ad Tuendam Fidem* (1998) felt obliged to 'protect the faith of the Catholic Church against the errors [. . .] above all of those who are specifically dedicated to theological disciplines'.
35. *Instructio de Synodis diocesanis agendas*, n. IV, AAS 89 (1997), 706–27.
36. According to n. 20, for the joint exercise of their pastoral ministry in conference to be 'legitimate and ruling on the several bishops, there must be intervention of the supreme Authority of the Church, which, through its universal law or through particular mandates, entrusts selected questions to the deliberation of the episcopal conference'.
37. N. IV, art. 12: 'For the doctrinal deliberations of the conference of bishops to be able to form an authentic magisterium and to be published, it is necessary for them to be approved unanimously by the member bishops, or for them, having been approved in plenary session by at least two thirds of the prelates with a deliberative voice, to obtain the approval (*recognitio*) of the Holy See.' This is the only requirement for unanimity in current canon law.
38. Since the *recognitio* will ensure that 'the doctrinal response' of the bishops 'will not prejudice interventions of the universal magisterium, but will rather prepare them' (n. 22, *in fine*).
39. Expressed thus *brevitatis causa* and to show that the teachings analyzed here do not involve faith as such, even if they cannot be treated lightly.
40. According to Cardinal de Lubac: 'A universal Church, prior to, or supposedly existing outside all the particular Churches, is no more than a creation of reason': *Les Églises particulières dans l'Église universelle*, Paris 1971, p. 54. He received support from, e.g., Cardinals Congar and Kasper.
41. Thus, n. 54: 'As is clear to all, there are numerous bishops who, while carrying out properly episcopal tasks, are not at the head of a particular Church.' They

make up 43% of the episcopate, many of them ordained absolutely, despite canon 6 of Chalcedon.

42. Cf. K. Delahaye, Ecclesia mater *chez les Pères des trios premiers siècles* (*Unam Sanctam* 46), Paris 1964.

43. The title of 'mater et magistra' of all the faithful means something different (see Lateran IV, cc. 2, 4, 5, 236; Lyon II, c. 1). Only Clement VI of Avignon (1342–5) claimed that 'the Roman [and not the universal] Church founded all the patriarchal, metropolitan, and cathedral Churches and all the dignities of every order existing within them. To her pastor and master, the Roman pontiff, is due the full ordering of all the Churches, dignities, offices and ecclesiastical benefices.' Rinaldi, *Annales*, vol. 25, p. 350.

44. N. 10: 'The universal Church is not the sister but the mother of all the particular Churches.'.

45. Nicetas of Nicomedia replied in 1136 to Anselm of Havelberg, who wrote to him from 'Rome, the most holy mother of us all': 'We do not refuse the Roman Church the primacy among its sisters' (see PL 118, 1217 and 1219); the patriarch John X Camatros replied thus to Innocent III: 'Where do you find that Christ said in the holy Gospels that the Church of the Romans is a universal mother? [. . .] The Church of the Romans holds the first rank among sisters, equal in dignity, born of the same Father' (PL 214, 757).

46. Of the thirty-odd ecclesiologies that have expressed themselves on the subject, only one seems convinced: figures established mainly after A. Cattaneo, 'La priorità della Chiesa universale sulla Chiesa particolare', *Antonianum* 77 (2002), 503–39.

47. 'Zur Theologie und Praxis des bischöflichen Amtes', in W. Schreer and G. Steins (eds), *Auf neue Art Kirche sein. Wirlichkeiten-Herausforderungen-Wandlungen*, Munich 1999, p. 44.

48. There is an excellent summary of this three-stage debate in K. McDonnell, 'The Ratzinger–Kasper Debate: The Universal Church and the Local Churches', *Theological Studies* 63 (2002), 227–50.

49. A specific example: in France, ordinations have been declining for seventy years. For years only one new priest per diocese has been ordained; in ten years, there will be a maximum of ten priests in each. Exhortations to put a universally viable model into practice have had no effect.

50. In *Le nouveau peuple de Dieu* (1971, pp. 65–9; 141–3 in German original), Ratzinger showed himself open to this view. In fact the collegiality of the 1983 Code, by dissociating the college of bishops from the communion of Churches, produced an unworkable innovation, a college of 4,500 bishops endowed with a false equality unrelated to the relative size and the problems of the Churches. Ratzinger himself had challenged this universalist conception beforehand and already pointed out 'the capital importance' of regional collegiality, which does not mean national: cf. 'La collegialité, développement théologique', in G. Baraúna (ed.), *L'Église de Vatican II*, Paris 1966, p. 786.

51. At the 2001 Consistory, Card. Silvestrini wished for 'more space for the authority of particular Churches and more confidence in them; this is necessary for good government', *Il Regno* 46 (2001), 12, 363.
52. After having cited H. Dombois, 'History teaches us that the unity of the Church and the unitary Church are so mutually contradictory that a unitary Church cannot be the model for the unity of the Church' ('Geschichtliche Kirchenspaltung und Einheitsproblematik', in *Begenung der Christen. Festschrift O. Karrer*, 2d ed. 1960, p. 395), Ratzinger himself could write that 'The image of a centralized State, which the Catholic Church herself presented until the Council, does not follow from the charge laid on Peter [. . .]. Unitary church law, unitary liturgy, unitary assignment of Episcopal sees based on the Roman centre – all these are things that do not necessarily form part of the primacy as such': *Le nouveau peuple* . . . , p. 68. He again refers to Dombois, p. 124.

The Signs of the Times

JOSÉ COMBLIN

The 'signs of the times' were understood by John XXIII and the Council in two different senses which are not always clearly distinguished. The relationship between the two is still somewhat indistinct. In the first place, the signs of the times indicated events and situations in contemporary Western society: that is, the changes taking place in society. How and why these changes could be taken as signs is what I shall go on to examine. In the second place, there is a reference to Matthew 16.4, so to eschatological signs, signs of the presence of the kingdom of God in this world. The Council documents and the Pope's speeches tended to conflate the two senses, as though the changes taking place in society had an eschatological meaning. How could this be possible? How was it psychologically possible to associate the two senses and so to find signs of the kingdom of God in social changes?

This seems not to have been a problem at the time. They were apparently not aware of any possible distance between the two concepts. Today it is precisely this that presents us with a problem. At that time they interpreted the signs of the times in the sense that the Church had to abandon the dream of Christendom and adapt to the new society. But why should it adapt to the new society? What seemed to cause no problem then does cause us a problem now.

The general intention behind the Council's use of the term 'sign of the times' leaves no room for any possible doubt. The Council wished to acknowledge that history existed, that the Church was in history, that the times of Christendom had now gone, and that the Church should open itself to the modern world. For centuries the Church had condemned the modern age in the hope of one day going back to Christendom. Today it is in the process of accepting the real situation: a new world exists. In the overall sense, this is quite clear.[1]

What is not quite so satisfying is the theology used to support this option. Why appeal to the biblical concept of 'signs of the times'? The signs of the times referred to eschatology. Would acceptance of and adaptation to the modern world fall within Christian eschatology? In what sense?

The concept of 'sign' is varied. Two different poles of its meanings can be distinguished:

I. Signs as warnings

The first meaning of 'sign' is 'alarm' or 'warning': to give a sign and draw attention to or demonstrate the presence of an unperceived but important reality. This is the meaning implied in Pope John's speeches, which launched the theme. The signs were situations, facts, structures that demonstrated a change in the world, which had to be taken into account, because it could imply a danger; this new reality required a response.

The introduction of the concept of sign clearly implicitly supposed that the Church could change and that changes in the Church could be justified by changes in the world. These changes could be related to changes in the world. Up until then the dominant view had been that the Church does not change and remains above the changes in the world, that it must close in on itself in order not to be contaminated and not be tempted to change also.

What were these signs of the times? What was it that raised an alarm, produced a call to pay attention and even to change course? This is not made clear, but we can picture the process. The sign was that the Church had lost the leadership of Christendom, that society was no longer subject to the dictates of the Church. Of course that had obvious for a long time: since the sixteenth century, Catholic monarchs had only been keeping up appearances. They were very religious and carried out totally un-Christian policies under the guise of excessive religion. The clergy went along with this because they depended on an alliance with the rulers to control society or to maintain the illusion that Christendom still existed. Then came the French Revolution, which was interpreted as a passing disturbance that could not last. All they had to do was hold out, stand firm, and everything would return to normal. The Church would win back its power. This was the concept in the nineteenth century. Vatican II came to shred these illusions: Christendom would not come back, and the Church would have to live with the modern world.

In Brazil the illusion of re-making a new Christendom was all too visible. When the coming of the Republic in 1889 brought about the separation of State from Church, the bishops and clergy did not understand this situation as a call to change. They did not see the sign, or saw a sign saying that they could not change and must not let themselves be carried along on a wave of changes. What they had to do was resist and wait for this new society based in the Republic to die of its own accord, destroyed by its inner corruption. If the Church had lost its dominion of the world, this was only a transitional phase, passing, like the persecutions under the Roman Empire, and resistance would prepare the Church for fresh glories. This was the prevailing theory.

II. Signs as pointers

In its second meaning, the sign of the times shows the course to be followed and the changes that need to be made. John XXIII took 'signs of the times' also and perhaps primarily in this sense. This was because he saw the contemporary world – modernity, that is – as having positive elements. The social changes taking place were not purely negative. We had to look at the world with greater optimism, which, for him, meant with greater objectivity.

The trouble is that consideration of the modern world does not in itself constitute a sign in the sense meant by John XXIII. It can lead to just the opposite approach. All John's predecessors since the French Revolution had viewed the modern world as the enemy and the tempter. Also, consideration of the decreasing power of the Church was not in itself a sign, because this decrease could be interpreted in other ways. It was an oppressed Church, reduced to a small remnant, but this remnant held the promise of a great future. This was how it had been interpreted in some conservative circles ever since the French Revolution.

Following John XXIII's line, the majority of Council Fathers tried to appreciate the positive elements in modernity. They surveyed the changes in the modern world and passed a favourable judgment on its projects and on many of its achievements, though they also drew attention to problems that remained unresolved or regretted the reduced space that was left to the Church. *Gaudium et Spes* made a list of the changes brought by modernity. This was not a scientific sociological exposition, but it did, without pretending to any strict criteria, set out its most visible aspects: science and scientific reasoning, economic development, social change, human rights – all seen in an optimistic light that corresponded to the view of the world that predominated among the Christian Democrat parties of the period. *Gaudium et Spes* was a document drawn up within a Christian Democracy environment. It recognized the liberal freedoms and the democracy proposed by the Welfare State, implying a capitalism tempered by the social laws imposed by the Social Democrat and Christian Democrat majorities in Europe. This model clearly seemed to be the one that should be spread to those 'backward' European countries that had not yet achieved it – Spain and Portugal. Implicit in it was that class struggles could be outdated by the Welfare State.

All this corresponded to the view of the leaders of the 'progressive' episcopate of Western Europe. At the same time, it was precisely in these countries that the Churches were losing power. Nevertheless the conciliar majority accepted explicitly or implicitly that the problem was the Church's failure to adapt to this situation of moderate modernity. This was why this situation of the Western world was taken as a sign. It was a sign that something was not going well in the Church and that the solution should be sought in a better adaptation to modern society, accepting many of its values.

The conservatives believed that all problems came from the world and that evil resided in the world and therefore the Church had to struggle against the contemporary world. As an argument they were able to invoke the fact that the Church's difficulties were arising precisely in those countries that had accepted the modern world. Where the Church had remained attached to Christendom, as in Spain and Portugal, nearly all the inhabitants were still faithful to observance of all the commandments of the Catholic Church. Yet the dominant party, which was that of northern Europe, held that the trouble was with the Church, which had failed to adapt. Its members believed that the situation of the modern world, which was producing problems for the Church, was an alarm signal, and that it was also a signal pointing in the direction to be followed: taking stock of the values of modernity and collaborating with it.

Was this position inspired by the gospel, or by the desire to regain the power lost in Western society? Was the Church of the bishops of Vatican II seeking to follow the gospel or to restore the lost power to the Church? The answer is not so clear. We might think that John XXIII himself was more inspired by evangelical motivations, but the same cannot be stated with certainty of all the leaders of the majority at the Council. The problem is that they were so convinced that the Church's cause was the gospel cause and that promoting the Church meant proclaiming the gospel, that they were not conscious of what really motivated them. There has to be a very strong suspicion that the motivation of the conciliar majority was the same as that of the minority: this was the triumph of the Church, the salvation of the Church; the two sides differed over the method but had the same objective.

How should we understand the interpretation of social changes as signs of the times, that is, as an eschatological sign, a sign of the coming of the kingdom of God? It was not the social and cultural situation in itself, modernity as such, that could have the value of an eschatological sign. Modernity as such has nothing to say about this. It simply exists, and it can be understood in many different ways – or indeed simply exist without being given any interpretation.

What was it that enabled modernity to be viewed as a sign of the times? It could have been an evangelical illumination, a Christian inspiration. Or it could have been a concern over the future of the Church. This is not clear in the council documents. The source could have been evangelical or it could have been institutional, as a sign to the institution's survival instinct. All organizations, all institutions, have to pay attention to signs of change that might oblige them to alter their own agendas. Could this have been what happened, or was it really an evangelical inspiration? What complicated the matter is that the bishops' understanding of the gospel was implicit, hidden, unconscious, and that they were all used to putting forward an edifying vision of their projects and of their decisions in order to live up to the demands of their profession. We cannot trust their public utterances because these express the image bishops wish to convey of themselves, conforming to the position they occupied in society. Their ongoing concern is the success of the Church. The permanent and strict control exercised by Rome over local Churches is essentially geared to this aspect. A bishop is never asked if the gospel is alive in his diocese but only about quantifiable results.

If we take the signs of the times in the evangelical sense – in the eschatological sense, that is – the signs of the times are apparent in all ages: signs of the great transformation of the world of the devil's kingdom into the kingdom of God. In every period we have to read the signs of the times and try to interpret these signs so as to know what to do at the present time in order to usher in the times proclaimed by Jesus. These signs of the times do not refer specifically to modernity, because they are present in all times.

It would seem that John XXIII used the expression 'signs of the times' in this evangelical or eschatological sense when he said that now was the 'time for the medicine of mercy rather than that of severity' and condemnations, and when he said that cultural forms, cultural clothing, had to be adapted to the new culture of the world. He thereby relativized all the cultural clothing the Church had acquired during previous centuries.

Was the Pope perhaps trying to say that there have been periods in which it was necessary to condemn and that there have been times in which a culture in total disaccord with that of the surrounding culture was needed? This was not the case. His opening speech might seem at first sight to imply this, but this is clearly not what he had in mind. At no time could the gospel be made to justify the Inquisition, the crusades against heretics, and so forth. At no time did the gospel ever express a need to stay within a particular culture, even if this meant forming a counter-culture embedded in society.

What, then, was the Pope thinking? He was thinking that in these times of change there was an opportunity for the Church to turn back to living the gospel. He meant to say that we had to take advantage of the moment of insecurity and indecision, that moment when the Church was not sure of being on the right path, in order to recall the gospel of Jesus, which is of mercy and service to people, not of imposition. Clearly however as pope, he could not say so in so many words. It would mean saying that for ages the Church had not been following the way of Jesus. No pope could confess as much.

So he was saying, therefore, that the Church had now reached the time for turning back to the gospel of Jesus. He meant to say that there are times when openings are made, when some changes are possible, and that the gospel can take advantage of such moments. There are times when the ecclesiastical institution can be better guided by the gospel. He knew that this is not always possible but that at that time there was a possible point of entry for the gospel.

Such moments do exist. In Brazil, as I have said, we missed an opportunity. When the separation of State and Church was brought about, in 1889, the hierarchy was surprised and perplexed. Then a famous missionary, Fr Julio Maria, the first Brazilian Redemptorist, made his voice heard. Julio Maria had been a brilliant lawyer before becoming a religious at the age of forty-seven. He then made a reputation as a famous orator and gained great prestige in society. Fr Julio Maria wrote and taught that this separation of Church from State was a grace from God and a sign: once the Church was independent of the State, it should recognize that the true Christians were the poor and should turn its activities toward them instead of looking to the powerful for its salvation. He discovered a sign of the times. But, as we know, the bishops were not prepared even to think on these lines, and they devised a programme to win back lost power using the rights the Republic offered all its citizens. They did not know how to discern the signs of the times.

III. Signs of the times in Matthew 16.3

All indications are that John XXIII meant to refer to the signs of the times in Matthew 16.3. The times of which Pope John spoke were not specifically those of the modern age, meaning the predominant culture of our time. He was alluding in the first place to eschatological times. He meant to say that we are in the time of the coming of the kingdom of God, a kingdom of mercy, appealing to all. At the same time, he judged that the historical moment was opportune for proclaiming the signs of the kingdom of God. This is why the

Pope did not seek to undertake an exegesis of the text of Matthew 16.3, which was not his task. Nevertheless, it is interesting to try to explain what is involved in the signs of the times of which Jesus spoke.

The context is the struggle of the authorities against Jesus. They are expecting the coming of a Messiah who will confirm them in their power and their privileges. Jesus denounces these authorities by saying that they 'cannot interpret the signs of the times'. What times does he mean? The messianic times, evidently. Jesus proclaims the arrival of the kingdom of God. There will be no more temple, and no more law, nor holiness acquired through human means.

The signs of the times show that the time of the ruling powers and of their whole religious order is over. There is no more time for this order, which they want to preserve because it assures them of staying in power. Jesus knows two times, radically opposed to one another. There is the time of the present religious system and the time of the kingdom of God. Jesus does not mean these new times to herald the end of the world. The new times are those that separate us from the end of the world and in which Jesus' way takes the place of the law which the ruling authorities made a power and a privilege.

This text influenced the thinking of John XXIII. He too proclaimed the end of one era with its whole content and the beginning of a new period. This new period is not new in the absolute sense. It has the newness of Jesus and of his way. The new period is the beginning of the time of Jesus. There is nothing to indicate that John XXIII was thinking of the religion of Jesus' adversaries or that he was making a comparison between that order and the order that prevailed in the Catholic Church. Nevertheless, he proclaimed new times, and these new times are precisely the times defined by Jesus. The analogy between the order of the adversaries of Jesus and the Catholic order of previous centuries must have been implicit in the structure of his thought, even though he cannot have been explicitly conscious of this analogy. If he had been conscious of it, it would hardly have been politic for a pope to allude to it in an official discourse.

Both John XXIII and the Council repeat *usque ad sacietatem* that the new thing they are claiming to bring in does not change any of the basic structures of the Catholic Church. They always avoid any allusion to institutional changes, and they stress that the institution must remain unchanging. It was clear that the conservative faction was very strong and that it intimidated both the bishops and the pope. Neither the pope nor the bishops wished to challenge this faction. They gave the impression that they were trying to convince themselves that some superficial changes in doctrine and changes in personal relationships could provide a response to the signs of the times. The Council was very fearful and very timid because the conservative faction was very strong, very arrogant, and very vocal. The majority thought they had to make innumerable concessions in order to make it accept a few superficial changes, which changed nothing in the structure of the Church and did nothing to alter the total domination of the clergy over the laity – the Christian people, that it. The reformers achieved far less than they thought. All the same, the Council was a first step and provided a support to all those in the Church who were seeking a return to the gospel of Jesus over the head of the whole bureaucratic edifice built up over centuries. But it was a step that still fell far short of the hopes of the Christian people.

IV. The Council texts on the signs of the times

The Council's references to the signs of the times are still very ambiguous. They are to be found in *Gaudium et Spes* 4a, 11a, and 44b; *Presbyterorum ordinis* 9b; *Unitatis redintegratio* 4a; *Apostolicam actuositatem* 14c. The text that seems to have guided the others, even though two of them do not speak of 'signs of the times' but use equivalent expressions, is that of GS 4a.

Its basic sense is that the signs of the times are the contemporary world, the modern world, the new situation of the world, the sum total of the phenomena of the contemporary world with its achievements and its problems. The signs are presented as though they were objective facts in a world situated outside the Church and could be considered objectively. The light of faith would arrive to shed light on this sum total of given facts. Why give a sociological study the name of signs of the times? They probably become signs of the times in the view of the faith that judges them. But how can faith judge a historical situation, as though it could have an objective view when looking at a world situated outside it?

There are, effectively, some problems. In the first place, the description of the modern world cannot be objective. We cannot stand outside the world in such a way that we can look at the world with indifferent eyes. We are part of the world, as is the Church and as are all men and women. Consequently we all judge in the light of our place in the world's history. Every view of the world is subjective. Now, the description the Council gave of the modern world and of its problems was the vision of the European bourgeoisie, of the Social Democrat and Christian Democrat parties. It was the vision of those who were basically in agreement with the ruling order. Without realizing it, the bishops were ideologically steered by the dominant political parties in Western Europe at that time. They failed to see that the vision of the world provided in *Gaudium et Spes* is ideological, represents the views of a particular party, and cannot claim scientific objectivity. In this way the bishops failed to see that they were simply legitimating the political regime of Western Europe. They were not concerned with the rest of the world, or with relations between Western Europe and the rest of the world, except in a very marginal fashion and through a Western projection of these relations.

Without realizing it, the bishops were impregnated with the outlook of the bourgeoisie of capitalist society, essentially in its Western European version. The Council adopted the outlook of the bourgeoisie of its time. The description it gave of contemporary society already contained a judgment, had already taken sides. It contained both judgment and action plan. The light of faith was no longer needed because another light had already judged society. We might say that the light of faith comes after seeing. But it is already captive, already biased, because the judgment has already been made in the act of seeing. The Council Fathers had not the least inkling of this because they formed an isolated club, immune to consideration and critique. If they had offered their document for critique by the intellectuals of the period, they would have been warned and would have seen that they were being spokesmen for an ideology.

The second difficulty is correlative to the first. What is this faith that is passing judgment? What is the light it is going to shine on the world? The Council Fathers seemed to suppose that the light of faith was their opinion, or their project, the way in which they interpreted Christianity. In any case, they give no explanation, as if this were self-evident, as though everyone knew what the faith that judges the world is and what the principles that guide this judgment are.

Besides this, everything is presented as though the light of faith could provide a solution to every element of the social question, so resolving all the contradictions of modern society or at least making a contribution to their resolution. There would be a light that would disclose a solution to each refractory element. In practice things do not work like this. The Church was not proposing anything original; it was merely putting forward Christian Democrat and Social Democrat proposals.

If one tries to learn what specific agenda *Gaudium et Spes* was putting forward, one has to recognize that it contributed nothing new and repeated what everyone was saying. The light of faith was unable to provide anything that was original or might offer guidance to the modern world. In the end, the teaching on the signs of the times boiled down to acceptance of the modern world. The Church renounced the plan to re-shape the old Christendom, accepted that conditions were no longer right for this, and decided to accept this society, which meant legitimizing the system of democracy prevailing in Western Europe. The Council reiterated what makes up or is called the social teaching of the Church. Unknowingly, it became the tool of Western bourgeois society.

It is impossible to underestimate this outcome. At least the hierarchy abandoned the dream of re-fashioning Christendom. These council documents are still important in our days, after a pontificate that did everything possible to re-fashion a new Christendom on the basis of the resources and instruments presented by modernity itself. This is the Opus Dei agenda: using modernity to re-fashion Christendom. It is the opposite of what the Council proposed. The Council's purpose was that the Church should cease condemning all the new elements brought by ongoing modernism and recognize what was of value in it – adopt a positive attitude, in other words, contrary to the Roman approach in Pope John Paul II's pontificate. This is why what the Council left is a considerable legacy. What it did not foresee was that the Church would return to its previous ways so soon.

At the Council there was a beginning of listening to the actual world. The world it heard was that of the European bourgeoisie of the time, but the fact of listening was in itself a great step forward. One also has to recognize that the bourgeoisie of that time was not as savage, as dominating, as hypocritical, and as indifferent to the sufferings of the world as the bourgeoisie of today. Today the Christian Democrat society the Council knew is in the process of disintegration and is being replaced by a globalized society in which no one controls the owners of money. All the Church can do is recognize that it no longer has any power in this new society. It can be used by the owners of money, but it cannot influence them. We already need another Council to say what the Church should do in a society that accords it no value.

Conclusion

By way of conclusion, allow me to put forward a different interpretation of the signs of the times. The disappointing fact is that *Gaudium et Spes* and the Council as a whole were a long way from giving the poor the recognition they should have by virtue of the Gospels and the New Testament in general. The central space is occupied by modernity – by development, that is. The overall impression is that the bishops fell into the trap of the ideology of development. They saw poverty as an accident of evolution and development as the solution to it. The real problem of poverty was a long way from their concerns, and only a small minority tried to introduce this problem, without succeeding. The small minority who were concerned with this matter never managed to make their message understood. Conditions were clearly not right for this to happen.

My starting point is the question of the light of faith. If what the light of faith is is not made explicit, nothing will be achieved and faith will simply confirm the established order, complementing it with pious exhortations. Now the light of faith is clearly apparent in the New Testament. Faith does not consist in intellectual acceptance of specific truths drawn from the Bible. Faith consists in recognizing God's plan, or the coming of the kingdom of God. It is a matter of recognizing the march of the people of God in our times.

The kingdom of God is not a situation or an institution; it is a movement. More precisely, the kingdom of God is the movement of liberation from the oppression to which some human beings subject other human beings by means of violence, deceit, lies, and so forth. The coming of the kingdom of God is a struggle against human forces and human institutions that are oppressive.

Jesus challenged a basic expression of domination: religious domination. A caste of priests, learned men and great landowners was dominating the people by means of a religion invented by them and presented as the word of God. Jesus' life was a struggle to free his people from the rule of lies, of injustice, of violence. Jesus came to draw back the veil, to expose the lie. Jesus was not battling against a mysterious sin hidden in the depth of individual conscience. Jesus battles against a sin that has forenames and surnames, that is very real and has very real institutions: the temple, the priesthood, the law.

The clearest illustration of this is in John, chapter 8. But all the gospels recount this struggle carried on by Jesus and, with it, the advance of the reign of God. In his humanity Jesus was a limited being and could not challenge all the oppressions of history. He chose the most significant one, the most disguised and hidden one: religious domination. This is the most dangerous, because it invokes God's authority.

According to Paul, the new times consist in the struggle of the Spirit against the law. He established this struggle between the Spirit and the law as a law of history in the death and resurrection of Jesus. Jesus, being a human creature, could take on only a small part of the struggle between sin and the kingdom of God, between the lie of the rulers and the struggle for emancipation of the ruled. After him, the same struggle goes on, but the circumstances change and domination shows itself in different forms. It is no longer a matter of literally beginning over again. The law denounced by Paul disappeared as that particular historical manifestation, but it is present in other forms in the world of today. Today there are other forms of domination and destruction of life, and there are other forms of struggle against this social sin, sin of the world – institutional sin too.

The light of faith reveals the actual presence of Jesus' same struggle in each moment of history. It does not simply indicate situations: it shows the advance of the kingdom of God against such powerful enemies. The signs are the struggles of the poor, the excluded, the dominated. Because that is where God is. Jesus is there, and we have to discover his presence in our world. The dominating powers deny their domination, hide the reality, make pretty speeches to justify and consolidate their domination. Jesus came to remove their masks and to reveal the truth to the world.

The light of faith shows what is really there but which the sciences, the communications media, and the prevailing narratives seek to deny or to hide. The signs of the times show what is happening in the world but which remains hidden because people wish to hide it, not because there is any mystery about it. The sin of the world is no mystery: it is highly visible to the victims, even if the privileged deny its existence. It s not a matter of discovering what is happening in an objective way by following official pronouncements, as *Gaudium et Spes* was still doing. The light of faith is what dissipates the darkness of sin. It reveals not the workings of society but the secret motivations that its structures try to hide. The opposite of light is not ignorance but darkness. The light of faith should not show people what they do not know; it should make plain to them what they are trying to hide.

The signs of the times at the time of the Council were the struggles of the oppressed for their liberation. They should have shown where Jesus was and where his adversaries were and where the struggle between them was taking place. They should have shown where the poor, the excluded, and the oppressed were and where the liberation movement of the kingdom of God was. A small minority knew that this should have been the case. But the overwhelming majority did not even know what was at stake. They had an exclusively religious view of Christianity and they had not understood the gospel. This is why most of them held an optimistic, ideological view of the world, the view of the European bourgeoisie.

Let this be a warning for a possible future council. What matters to Jesus is not scientific and technological progress, or economic and social changes. What concerns him is the liberation of the oppressed. And this is a subject that is more pressing today than at any other time.

Translated by Paul Burns

Note

1. The most complete study of the signs of the times in Vatican II is Clodovis Boff, *Sinais dos tempos. Princípios de leitura*, São Paulo 1979. The commentaries written directly after the Council all present a euphoric picture, an expression of the feelings experienced in the early years following it.

III. The Future of Vatican II

The Theological Options of Vatican II: Seeking an 'Internal' Principle of Interpretation

CHRISTOPH THEOBALD

How should we interpret a 'substantial' body of texts, which takes up very nearly a third of the very latest edition of the documents of the twenty-one ecumenical councils? To borrow a well known phrase from Michel de Certeau, the Council Fathers might be said not to have been afraid to 're-invent Christianity'. No subject escaped their attention: from Revelation to listening to the signs of the times, from marriage to international peace, from education and the communications media to ecumenical and interfaith dialogue, from the nature and mission of the Church to the redefinition of its various functions, ministries, and states of life, the bishops managed to depict a renewed vision of Christianity on a planet embarking on globalization, even to put forward a programme of reform that exceeds anything we might hare dared to imagine earlier. None of the twenty preceding councils showed so much daring and ambition: allowing a consensus to emerge among those more than two thousand prelates from all continents and obtain their agreement on the responses to be made to virtually all the questions facing the Church at the dawn of a new age for humanity – such is the absolutely unheard-of legacy of these great twentieth-century assizes.[1]

My purpose here is not to show how it was possible to reach agreement on such a broad scale, nor to inquire into the meaning of the Council's work over its course in time,[2] but to separate out the principle for interpreting its body of documents. The decisive significance of this question for the present stage of reception of the Council will come to light along the way.

To give the point some precision at the outset, we might evoke the distant analogy of the scriptures. Before, during, and after the Council both

Protestant and Catholic theology had raised the question of their internal unity, given the diversity of the theologies of the Old and New Testaments, brought out by two hundred years of historical research: 'Is the canon of the New Testament the basis of the unity of the Church?,' Ernst Käsemann asked in 1951, unleashing a lively debate on what he had called the 'canon of the scriptural canon'. No one would dare to claim that the council texts were inspired, even if there is a certain tendency in some ecclesial circles to give them that status. But we do need to ask ourselves not only *what the nature of the unity of the Council' work is, exactly* – and here the analogy between different Christian (or other) bodies of work could play a part – but also and above all *how, through a sort of reflexive turn, the* corpus *of Vatican II positions itself*, situating itself simultaneously in relation to the scriptures with their unique status and to tradition, and indeed to extra-textual authorities such as the name of Jesus and the work of the Spirit.

I. A hypothesis

In what follows I should like to reflect on the consequences deriving from the fact that this main question and others related to it, such as the relationship between revelation and faith, or between freedom and historical context ('signs of the times'), did not 'surface' until during the final session of the Council (autumn 1965) and then in the shape of a doctrinal compromise. What would have happened if the texts promulgated *before* the final adoption of *Dei Verbum, Dignitatis humanae, Ad gentes* and *Gaudium et spes* had been able to benefit from the foundations laid down, not without difficulty, by these documents? This question, which is not dependent on 'conciliar fiction' but recalls the history of the compilation of its documents, sheds light on the process of reception dating from the end of the Council. For forty years the Church has been greatly concerned with its states of life, ministries, and structures, as the long series of Roman Synods under John Paul II eloquently witnesses; it has also managed to re-define its relations with Judaism, with non-Christian religions, and with civil society. It is not so clear however that the intuitions of the Constitution on Revelation, for example, in particular the relationship this establishes with *the scriptures*, have received all the attention they deserve. We can then ask whether a more accurate understanding of the 'internal' principle of the *corpus* will not have repercussions on the *present-day* reception of the Council and the new – and doubtless more radical – 'thresholds' this will have to cross.

(a) Is the Church 'the main subject matter' of the Council?

If we look first at *the history of the compilation* of the texts, several facts emerge. Not the least difficulty the Council that met in October 1962 faced was cutting a few breaks through the vast forest of the seventy-odd preparatory schemas, leading to an overall vision that could be defined very gradually and with constant reference to the principle John XXIII himself had laid down for the Council in his opening speech, *Gaudet Mater Ecclesia*. This principle, which is generally called the principle of 'pastorality of doctrine',[3] rejected the classic distinction between doctrine and discipline or dogma and heresy that had very largely guided the preparatory work. It is therefore easy to see that it was received very differently depending on the outlooks of the Council Fathers. So this internal process of reception, which went on throughout the four sessions of the Council, opens up a whole range of possibilities on the level of the course of debates, which could either remain more or less independent of a collective adherence to the principle or, on the contrary, derive from it.

During the first session the assembly was therefore looking for its direction. The pastoral debate on the liturgy – an area that transcends the classic distinction between doctrine and discipline – was followed by the first major confrontation on the subject of interpretation of the Faith (the *traditum*, as Yves Congar called it), which was then carried on in the mixed Commission set up on 21 November to provide a way out of the impasse brought about by the preceding day's vote on *De fontibus* (on the sources of revelation). Everything suggests that this major conflict, which seemed insurmountable at the time, served to strengthen the position of those who were trying to get round it by shifting the conciliar debate toward the bearers of tradition, the *tradentes*. This was then the ecclesiological orientation that had the upper hand from the end of the first session. We have to recognize that it corresponded to the expectation of the majority of the Fathers, that it was upheld in John XXIII's pre-council address, *Ecclesia Christi lumen gentium* (11 Sept.), and that it was above all at the centre of the Belgian strategy, powerfully orchestrated by Cardinal Suenens, set out by him on 4 December,[4] and strengthened the next day by Cardinal Montini, the future Pope Paul VI.[5] Prepared for well in advance, these two days in fact decided the fate of the Council: *the Church became its 'main subject matter'*.[6]

The main questions of fundamental theology however abandoned for a time only, returned progressively at the end of 1963 and were considered above all in the last two sessions (autumn 1964 and 1965), giving rise to varying formulations in texts of different provenance and status. Differing outlooks first became apparent in respect of the 'ecumenical' idea of 'reform' and its doctrinal dimensions; they reappeared later in discussion of how to integrate the historical and cultural position of the recipients of the gospel into the pastoral shape of doctrine itself. Finally, the teaching authority's task of interpretation, where a balance seemed to have been struck at the time of the debate on the schema *De Ecclesia* (LG 25) was again challenged by unprecedented questions such as that of religious freedom, stripping bare, so to speak, divergent views on the subject of the underlying principle of Christian and ecclesial existence, *the transmission of revelation*. In most cases, compromises were reached by juxtaposing expressions or the use of deliberately open formulas. More precise formulations, such as those of *Gaudium et spes*, *Ad gentes*, and *Dignitatis humanae*, came too late to bring about a fresh look at the earlier texts; this in the end led to a sort of hermeneutical indecision that left the post-conciliar period heavily mortgaged.

How, then, should we evaluate the connections between the span of reception/non-reception of the principle laid down by John XXIII for the Council and the planning of its work? After the period of research, on 5 December 1962, a selection of twenty documents was distributed, and a new Co-ordinating Commission was set up, entrusted with the planning of future work. It was on account of the bias in that Commission that the Suenens project was able to succeed, all the more easily in that at the very first meeting the Belgian primate was given responsibility for *De Ecclesia* (which evolved into *Lumen gentium*) and Schema XIII, the future Constitution *Gaudium et spes*, the two texts that formed the main axis of his project. With hindsight, there is no denying that the planning of the work of the Council and the span of reception of the 'pastorality' principle became separated from that moment. Was there a chance that collective adherence to this principle could then have become the main influence on the compilation of the texts? This proposal, put forward by Cardinal Bea on 15 October 1962 to the Secretariat for Extraordinary Affairs,[7] was probably utopian, since it took no real account of the preparatory work already done and the logic of the conciliar programmes of Trent and Vatican I, based on the distinction between doctrine and discipline. Establishing a degree of independence between the 'work' of the principle and planning the Council's work programme starting from ecclesiological questions has important effects on our conception of the conciliar *corpus*: should its internal unity be found in *understanding of the Church*, stretched between the church's interior (*Lumen gentium*) and its exterior (*Gaudium et spes*), or rather in the *word of God* (*Dei Verbum*), received by the Church in the world of the time thanks to a new relationship – defined as 'pastoral' – to the scriptures and to tradition?

At the time of the final vote on the Constitution *Dei Verbum*, on 29 October 1965, the *rapporteur* touched almost furtively on the place of this text in the Council's work, stating that it 'formed the very bond among all the questions dealt with by this Council. It sets us,' he declared, 'at the very heart of the mystery of the Church and at the epicentre of ecumenical considerations.' In autumn 1964 the Theological Commission had already noted that *De Revelatione* was 'in a way the first of all the Constitutions of this Council, so that its Preface introduces them all to a certain extent'.[8] That statement was however to remain a dead letter due to a fact of reception, i.e. that the Constitution on the Church in practice took the premier place among all the council documents;[9] this fact was favoured by Pope Paul VI and the way in which he presented the chief aims of the Council at the opening of the second session: 'If we set before our eyes, venerable brothers, the sovereign idea that Christ is our founder, our leader, invisible but true, that we receive everything from him, in such a way as to form, with him, the "total Christ" of whom St Augustine speaks and with whom the theology of the church is completely filled, we can better understand the aims of this Council, which, for the sake of brevity and for easier understanding, we shall present under four headings: the understanding, or, if you prefer, the consciousness of the Church; its renewal; the re-establishment of the unity of all Christians; the Church's dialogue with the men of today.'[10] Against this background, it seems significant that when *Dei Verbum* was promulgated, on 18 November 1965, the pope said nothing further about the fundamental significance of this Constitution but saw the post-conciliar period rather from an institutional point of view. Everything suggested that the page had already been turned.

(b) *The ecclesiological orientation of the reception*

Looking now more directly at the *history of the reception* of the *corpus*, we cannot fail to see a confirmation of the ecclesiological orientation induced by Paul VI. Perhaps it was partly due to the theological consensus of the majority of the Fathers: unlike neo-Thomism, this consensus is inspired by a 'new theology' distantly along the lines of 'moderate traditionalism', more sensitive to a dogmatic-historical vision than to a dogmatic-juridical concept of Catholic Christianity; moulded by patristic culture, its proponents willingly relate to the romantic Tübingen school, the apologetics of Blondel, or again the transcendentalism of Jacques Maréchal. Attentive above all to tradition as the *historical conscience of the Church*, this multiform paradigm, also vulnerable to bipolar expressions of opposites (Church/world), left the questions of fundamental theology raised at the end of the Council somewhat in the shade.

It is in this context that the *difference of form* between the texts of Vatican I and those of Vatican II begin to emerge: while the very precise but incomplete nature of the 1870 text required a complete re-framing in a more global perspective (which was done at Vatican II in the setting of its ecclesiology), the texts of the latter Council pose great problems of interpretation, owing not only to their extent, as I have already said, but also to their polycentric structure, which is now becoming apparent.[11]

Those who despite everything are still attached to the unified vision of Catholic culture and its expression in the various papal pronouncements of the nineteenth and twentieth centuries will therefore find it tempting to mould the conciliar texts into a coherent system and to define their official reception according to the classical procedures of a still highly hierarchical and centralized Church. The *call for synthesis* began to be heard twenty years after the closure of the Council. Among theologians, in 1985 the Vatican historian H. J. Pottmeyer suggested an attempt at 'dialectical' division of its reception into periods, which became a school:[12] the task today would be to 'integrate what is obligatory in pre-conciliar theology with the new insight of an ecclesiology of communion and a Christian anthropology that requires a commitment in favour of human dignity'.[13] In the same year, the Synod that raised 'the ecclesiology of communion' to '*a central and fundamental concept in the documents of the Council*'[14] also expressed the wish that 'a catechism or compendium of all Catholic teaching' should be drawn up, a wish fulfilled in 1992. Before then, in 1983, and in the same spirit of ecclesial synthesis, John Paul II had promulgated the new Code of Canon Law.

Others see the polycentric and open nature of the collection of texts, with its appeal to 'the sense of faith' and to individual Churches, as implying moving into a *multiform practice* of renewal and reform, which willingly takes its inspiration from the spirit of the Council even if it cannot always quote its letter. Is this why the process of official reception, undertaken following the 1985 Synod, concentrates above all on 'states of life' and 'ministries': lay people, priests, religious, and bishops? The fraternal disagreement between Cardinal Kasper and the future Pope Benedict XVI over relations between individual Churches and the universal Church, certainly not provoked simply by the progress of ecumenical dialogue, again confirms the centrality of the ecclesiological viewpoint; even though the author of the 'Letter on Certain Aspects of the Church as Communion' (1992) recalled in 2000 that 'Vatican II clearly wished to inscribe discourse on the Church in and subordinate it to discourse on God' and reproached its reception with having 'neglected this qualifying aspect in favour of particular ecclesiological statements only'.[15]

There is, however, no denying that the Council also led to a deep revision of the Church's relations not only with Judaism but with the other world religions. It was in this context that the thorny question of mission was tackled afresh. At the same time, innumerable problems relating to society and more and more pointed ethical discernment arose and were subjected to anthropological and moral treatment. Vatican II was in fact followed by an unprecedented acceleration in the process of modernization: Western societies moved into the post-industrial era, and the system of economic, cultural, and religious exchange was rapidly globalized; the perverse effects of these changes began to make themselves felt, not only in the Third World but also in the Northern hemisphere. After the disappearance of the Iron Curtain, which had hung so heavy at the time of the Council and after, a new consciousness was developed, often called 'post-modern', characterized by a radical pluralism of cultures and a deep scepticism with regard to any claims to ultimate truth, as well as by the inevitable, more or less violent reactions brought about by this experience of general relativism.

In all this, the Church's relationship to the scriptures and tradition, also indeed the whole conception of Christian revelation and its place in the history of societies, were at stake, *but without really being put into words in themselves*.[16] It seemed as though the hermeneutical turning, so necessary in other respects, had made access to the question of truth difficult, and that the fragmentation and increasing complexity of the questions raised had progressively eroded the evangelical capacity for concentration. Instead of reacting by a fresh return to the 'principle' of faith, there was an insistence on community appurtenances,[17] and a part of the hierarchy tried to counter the threat posed by ultra- or post-modernity to the old Catholic culture by strengthening its doctrinal regulation, especially during the last decade of the second millennium.[18]

It was not until around the Jubilee that the question of the internal principle of the Council's *corpus* began to be considered *in its totality* as a 'sure compass by which to take our bearings in the century now beginning.'[19] In John Paul II's apostolic letter *Tertio millennio adveniente* (1994) we read: 'The Council's enormously rich body of teaching and *the striking new tone* in the way it presented this content constitute as it were a proclamation of new times. The Council Fathers spoke in the language of the gospel, the language of the Sermon on the Mount and the Beatitudes. In the Council's message God is presented *in his absolute lordship over all things*, but also as *the One who ensures the authentic autonomy of earthly realities.*'[20] And in his apostolic letter *Novo millennio ineunte* (2001) the pope devoted a very long argument to the course taken by the Nazarene according to the Gospels.[21]

The history of the *reception* of the Council itself takes us back to the history of the *drafting* of its body of texts, inviting us to raise afresh the question of the internal principle of their interpretation.

II. The principle of 'pastorality' and its reception by the Council

The way to approach this question is to start with John XXIII's opening speech, which introduced the terminology of 'pastorality' and then see what became of it in the composition of the council documents.

(a) Pastorality and ecumenicity

What is meant by this *pastorality*[22] extolled by the pope? Put in the simplest terms, the answer is this: there can be no proclamation of the gospel without taking account of its recipients; and, to define the position of the latter more clearly, we should add that 'what' is at stake in the proclamation is already at work in them, in such a way that they can accede to it in all freedom.

There is no doubt that Karl Rahner can take credit for being the first to point out, in the *Generalia* of his *Disquisitio brevis de Schemate 'De fontibus revelationis'* (Oct./Nov. 1962) and *Animadversiones de Schemate 'De ecclesia'* (end Nov.), the lack of pastoral style and ecumenical spirit in these two texts,[23] points later taken up by most of the Fathers in the majority camp. The great German theologian not only linked proposition of truth and *possible* reception (*indoles pastoralis*) but also, in a more specific fashion, Catholic proposition of truth and *possibility* of our separated brethren 'having a foreboding that we may be obscuring what they legitimately defend as true and properly belonging to them',[24] placing in that category the three disputed questions of fundamental theology that determine all the others: the pre-eminence of scripture, the discernment of what unities us in tradition, and the magisterium's obedience to the Word of God.

The representatives of the Secretariat for Christian Unity, Cardinal Bea, Bishop de Smedt, and Bishop Volk, who at the time crystallized the views of all those who opposed the preparatory schemas, seized on this internal link between pastoral and ecumenical form in the council documents to be composed. Among the three interventions by Bishop Volk, I recall that made at the end of the first session, which, in a sense, foreshadowed the definitive version of *Dei Verbum*. Volk noted that *De Ecclesia* 'has not enough *of the flavour of the gospel for the Catholic faithful, for those who are separated from us, and for the whole world*: dogmatic teaching on the Church itself should be put forward by the Council as Gospel, which means Good News; and it is in this way that dogmatic teaching is in itself truly *pastoral*. If teaching has no saving power in itself, pastoral work can no longer add this. This is the reason why the two must not be separated. Such evangelical teaching also serves *ecumenical* requirements at the same time. These in effect can never be satisfied by concessions, but only by propounding the faith the Church professes about itself in a manner as rich as in Sacred Scripture, which views the Church as an essential part of the saving work of God.'[25]

(b) The conciliar corpus: signs of a double hesitation

This is where the relationship between the Council and scripture came to the fore; it was nevertheless to remain controversial to the end. Once we become aware of the part played by the Unity Secretariat in the drafting of *Dei Verbum*, the importance of its opening formula, introduced by Bishop Volk on 1 October 1965, the course of its composition, as noted and commented above, and the central place given, from the end of the third session, to the Dogmatic Constitution on Divine Revelation, our first task is to search this text for signs of the conciliar reception of the principle of pastorality, henceforth linked to that of ecumenicity.

The Preface to *Dei Verbum*, which, according to the *rapporteurs*, introduces the body of the work, places the *doctrinal work* of the Council in the line of the Johannine *kerygma* (1 John 1.2–3), giving it its full weight but also recognizing that the *Word heard* by the successors of the apostles can never be proclaimed without an act of *interpretation*. What is introduced in this solemn opening is effectively codified at the end of the second chapter, on the transmission of revelation by the living teaching office of the Church, of which it is clearly stated: 'This teaching office is not above the word of God, but serves it' (DV 10). It is not until chapter 6, on 'Sacred Scripture in the Life of the Church', that the deep link between pastorality and ecumenicity is expressed, with all the clarity one could wish; precisely when this text puts scripture into the hands of *all* and guides teaching work toward its kerygmatic interpretation, taking particular care that pastoral ministry of the word stays rooted in 'the study of the sacred page [which] is, as it were, the soul of sacred theology' (DV 24). It seems to me that we are here in the presence of two sides of the principle sought, which introduces *a double hesitation* into the conciliar *corpus: it wishes to be understood as the* (historically situated) *trace* of a listening to the word of God, which, going through study of another body of texts, that of the inspired scriptures, is effectively inscribed in an interpretation of them (*traditum*); at the same time it *puts* the authorized interpreters – pastors, exegetes, and theologian – *in touch with everyone*, inviting them in their turn to embark on study of the scriptures for the sake of hearing the same word (see DV 21 and 25).

However, this – relational – principle, both programmatic and critical, is still largely formal. Even if John Paul II pointed to a 'new tone' in the texts and heard in them 'the language of the Gospel . . . and the Beatitudes',[26] it is still noticeable that relationship to the scriptures varies considerably from one council document to another, even if they were monitored by the Biblical Institute. But as yet no systematic research has been carried out on this point.[27] In its chapter 3, 'The Divine Inspiration and the Interpretation of Sacred Scripture', *Dei Verbum* very obviously accepts the indispensable role of critical exegesis and, in its section 12, details the two extremes of the act of interpretation: the historical context of the meaning, looked at on the basis of the nature of the text ('literary forms'), and respect for the 'content and unity' of the whole Bible (by analogy with the Faith). Without invalidating this insight, the present shift in the status of the Bible in European culture, the re-definition of relations between Christianity and Judaism, and the evolutions (historical and narrative or rhetorical) in the field of exegesis will no doubt continue to refine, if not to modify, the critical principle of the conciliar *corpus* and to re-frame some of its developments. I shall return to this later.[28]

(c) Relationship to tradition or the risk of hermeneutical indecision

Besides the fact that the work of critical exegesis and in particular the historicity of the Gospels (DV 19) remained very controversial to the end of the Council, the relationship of its teaching to scripture was itself subject to a degree of hermeneutical indecision, in that the debate on 'the constitutive nature of tradition' was never carried to any conclusion. All the questions come back here, and first that which bears on *the actual status of doctrine*: is the relationship between scripture and tradition really a problem of truths or of points contained in the 'deposit'? Is doctrine not rather *one* way of establishing, in different contexts, conditions under which the kerygmatic or pastoral event can be truly produced, in all its dimensions, at the very heart of tradition? This must be what John XXIII had in mind when he spoke of the 'forms and proportions of a magisterium which is predominantly pastoral in chracter' Depending on the choice one makes, interpretation of the Council texts will tend either toward a doctrinal and juridical synthesis or toward the idea of a set of rules allowing us to discern the kerygmatic and pastoral event that is continually and effectively being brought to pass among Christians and others in contact with the inspired scriptures.

The other question raised by reference to tradition bears on the *relationship between teaching and history*. In his opening speech, John XXIII had already expressed his absolute confidence in the presence of God in human history, which is still seen as completely autonomous, and God's attentiveness to human capacity for learning. 'Hermeneutical' attention to the *historical and cultural context* of the recipients and so to the cultural image of 'revealed truth' forms part of the principle of 'pastorality'. These two points just raised – the (in the end critical) role played by scripture in the interpretative tradition of the Church and the cultural situation of the recipients of the gospel – are in fact nerve centres in which, within a conciliar debate largely dominated by ecclesiological considerations, basic concerns keep recurring; these were to remain with the Council Fathers, especially from the start of the third session, without their finding unified formulations that would enable them to specify the relatively formal hermeneutics of *Dei Verbum*.

1. Concerning the first point, the debate on *the notion of 'reform'* is most significant and central. It was not until the end of the second session, in the discussion on ecumenism, that the distinction between *renovatio* and *reformatio* emerged. While the *relatio* of the schema understood *spiritual renewal*, in the spirit of Paul VI, only as conversion of the heart or holiness of life, Bishop de Provenchère extended it to worship, to institutions, and also to way doctrine is set out. Bishop Volk was the first to introduce the verb *reformare*: 'The more the Church shows its readiness *to reform itself* and to show its true nature more clearly, the more *credible* its witness becomes,'[29] These second session debates bore fruit in 1964, when the Dogmatic Constitution on the Church, *Lumen gentium*, and the Decree on Ecumenism, *Unitatis redintegratio*, were promulgated simultaneously, thereby juxtaposing two different perspectives: the more christo-ecclesial one of Paul VI and others who intervened, finally introduced into LG 8, and the more doctrinal and hermeneutical one, inherited from John XXIII and upheld, not to say developed, by Bishop Volk and others, which can be found in the final version of chapter 2 (sections 6 and 11) of the Decree on Ecumenism.

Starting from the poverty and oppression of Christ, *Lumen gentium* 8 makes a comparison between him and the Church, which it nuances at the end of the argument in order to bring in the concept of *renovatio*, without calling the holiness of the Church into question: 'While Christ, "holy, innocent, undefiled" (Heb. 7.26) knew nothing of sin (2 Cor. 5.21), but came to expiate only the sins of the people (cf. Heb. 2.17), the Church, embracing sinners in her bosom, is at the same time holy and always in need of being purified, and incessantly pursues the path of penance and renewal' (LG 8d). The beginning of section 6 of the Decree on Ecumenism seems to be cast in the same mould, but the introduction of the word *reformatio*[30] and the breadth of meaning given to it suggest quite another approach, while the quotation from Pope John XXIII's opening speech introduces, for the first time, the hermeneutical problem: 'Therefore, if the influence of events or of the times has led to deficiencies in conduct, in Church discipline, or even in the formulation of doctrine (*which must be carefully distinguished from the deposit itself of faith* [my italics]), these should be appropriately rectified at the proper moment' (UR 6b).[31]

We are here faced with a difference in doctrine of which the Council was probably not fully aware.[32] Is it resolved by the introduction of a 'hierarchy' of truths in the final version of *Unitatis redintegratio* 11? Not really, because this argument, certainly envisaging the internal unity of the mystery, but in a purely doctrinal sense, does not leave room for placing church tradition (with its different levels of expression) and the Christian Bible in a hermeneutical *and* critical relationship. It is highly significant that *Dei Verbum* does not come back to this point. This text, using the vocabulary of 'renewal' more openly, in its final version strengthens somewhat the regulatory function of scripture, notably weakened earlier, but without really understanding the ecumenical requirement for its critical role in relation to tradition.[33]

2. The *historical and cultural context of the recipients of the gospel* – the second point of controversy – came to the surface of conciliar consciousness in 1964 and, more particularly, dominated the debates in the last session on the Pastoral Constitution on the Church in the Modern World, *Gaudium et spes*. This question introduced a complication into the pastoral and ecumenical principle that had not been spotted at the beginning of the Council. The Fathers found it difficult to distinguish between questions of doctrinal *content* and the problem of the *form* of doctrine. The debates on the concept of 'world', on the relationships between redemption and creation, and on the crucial question of atheism threatened to hide the more basic difficulty of the historicity of all the declarations of faith. The *pluralism* this difficulty produced inevitably affected not only the diversity of denominations, which had already been considered, but also the relationship of the Catholic Church with non-Christian religions and with cultures, and among the latter especially modern culture, approached through the prerogatives of conscience and the religious freedom of the recipients of the gospel. These different approaches to the same question were often juxtaposed, without

the principle linking them becoming a subject of debate. This gave rise to a similar divergence of view to that encountered with the concept of *reformatio*.

Chapter 2 of *Lumen gentium*, on the People of God, re-introduced in October 1963, tackled the problem of pluralism from the angle of the catholicity of the *Church*: its section 13 is closely related to a new closing section 17 on the missionary nature of the Church,[34] and the two passages deal for the first time with the relationship between evangelization and cultures – the exchange between them brought about by the gospel – but without in any way reflecting on the repercussions of plurality of cultures on *the very interpretation of the gospel and of its doctrinal formulation*. From this point of view, *Lumen gentium* 44 takes a very different line, even though in its final version it refers back to *Gaudium et spes* 13; this development on catholicity seems then to be placed on this side of a sort of 'boundary', which not only split the work of the Council into two phases but also ushered in a distinction between two different sets of problems, leaving their intrinsic linkage still unresolved.

Gaudium et spes 44, on 'The help which the Church receives from the modern world', took final shape only very gradually. At the time of the first council debate on the future Pastoral Constitution, in October/November 1964, the question of culture had already been raised. But only Cardinal Lercaro made it the 'nub' of the text by once more linking the credibility of concern for the culture of the present time (and the future) to the Church's capacity for *reforming its own ecclesiastical culture*. At the beginning of the fourth session, history, seen more precisely in the shape of the present rapid rate of change and the great variety of cultures and ways of thinking, was recognized as a real theological setting. On this basis, the text introduced 'revealed truth' in a process of interpretation that bore *at the same time* on that and on the 'exceedingly various' languages of the present time. The final version, proposed only on 2 December 1965 by thirteen Fathers,[35] inserted an important passage into the text, indicating the extent of the hermeneutical problem in the way that section 44 had tried to express it from the beginning of the process of its redaction:

> For, from the beginning of her history [the Church] has learned to express the message of Christ with the help of the ideas and terminology of various peoples, and has tried to clarify it with the wisdom of philosophers, too. Her purpose has been to adapt the gospel to the grasp of all as well as to the needs of the learned, insofar as such was appropriate. Indeed, this accommodated preaching of the revealed Word ought to remain the law of

all evangelization. For thus each nation develops the ability to express Christ's message in its own way. At the same time, a living exchange is fostered between the Church and the diverse cultures of people.'[36]

The concern of this last insertion was to link the hermeneutical problems raised by John XXIII's opening speech and the 'sharing' ideas introduced into in LG 13, on the catholicity of the Church, though it did not in itself succeed in demonstrating their internal linkage. If we can then regard GS 44 as an ultimate re-reading – still, indeed, problematic – of LG 13, it also contains an analogous *reprise* of section 22 of the Decree on the Missionary Activity of the Church, which, while again citing LG 13, relies most heavily on its section 17, on the mission of the Church. The central portion of the text notably specifies the task of theology from a point of view that can be called hermeneutical:

> ... theological investigation must necessarily be stirred up in each major socio-cultural area, as it is called. In this way, under the light of the tradition of the universal Church, a fresh scrutiny will be brought to bear (*novae investigationi subiiciantur*) on the deeds and words which God has made known, which have been consigned to sacred Scripture, and which have been unfolded by the Church Fathers and the teaching authority of the Church.[37]

So within the course of the genesis of the Decree on the Missionary Activity of the Church, the ultimate task of undertaking a *fresh examination* of revelation *itself* is not passed over in silence. Note above all that the very balanced formulation tries to move beyond the dichotomy between form and content by stating that interpretation bears directly on the 'deeds and words which God has made known', while still accepting that we cannot access these except through reading the scriptures, explained by the Fathers of the Church and its teaching authority.[38] Furthermore, the text also suggests a way beyond the distinction – still quite marked – between faith and morals by pointing to a deeper adaptation of the gospel *over the whole spread of Christian life*. This section, which ends chapter 3 of the Decree, on 'Particular Churches', is the Council's last word on the hermeneutical problem.

In all the texts cited, reinterpretation of the gospel is treated in terms of 'adaptation', which keeps a degree of exteriority or an instrumental relationship between truth and historical context.[39] When the Council speaks of the modern context, it effectively seems to presuppose an already acquired body of doctrine, of which it needs only to clarify the anthropological implications; when it tackles the very interpretation of the gospel, it stays on the level of a set of programmatic declarations, without really linking them to the problem of knowledge of their context. This general post is the effective limit reached by the texts of the last session, showing that the Council did not achieve a clear and precise understanding of the hermeneutical problem, in its at once historical and systemic shape, which *envelops and articulates* interpretation of the context *and* that of the gospel. Even a man such as Bishop Volk, who saw how to raise the problem in relation to ecumenism, did not rise to the level of his earlier interventions during this last session.

(d) An 'internal' principle of interpretation

This concludes our survey of *conciliar* reception of the principle of 'pastorality', which from the first session was linked to that of ecumenicity. What conclusion can we draw from it for interpreting the body of texts as a whole? Even if we are finally left with a degree of hermeneutical indecision, the forty years of reception and progressive historicizing of the Council will have led us to the point where the significance of the principle, the decisions it implies (even those not taken by the Council), and the marks it left on the whole body of the texts are sufficiently intelligible to be reassessed and handed on to a new phase of reception.

The extreme complexity of the conciliar *corpus* and the fragmentation of the process of reception mean that we should first emphasize the great *simplicity of the principle* contained in it: the pastoral and kerygmatic relationship, always set in its history or culture, between those who proclaim the gospel and those who receive it through an uninterrupted process of 'handing on'. The pattern of communication, which *Dei Verbum* 2 bases on the very economy of revelation, not only implies a 'friendly' symmetry among all the 'actors' in the process of revelation but also indicates the conditions for making it credible – 'deeds and words having an inner unity' – which forbid any separation between the gospel and its interpretation (*traditum*) on one side and its authorized bearers or interpreters (*tradentes*) on the other.

Without being entirely informed by this principle – for reasons given above – the conciliar texts are as it were 'stretched' between scripture (which is a constant in all of them, mainly through their use of citations) and the multiplicity of cultural contexts of a world in the process of globalization. They seek to 'regulate' the hermeneutical and critical relationship between these two poles, as they do the relational play between *hermeneutes* and other players. Their ecclesial 'substructure' (unilaterally favoured in their reception) is to be found on this – sacramental: see LG 1 – trajectory between the Good News of God, heard in the scriptures, and its innumerable recipients; this very trajectory also provides the texts with their theologal *raison d'être* and the root of their unity in plurality. Insofar as they are 'regulatory' texts, the conciliar documents are necessarily rooted *in history* (which we are constantly in danger of forgetting): their *modern positioning* of conscience and freedom – the freedom of every act of faith and reception in the first place – shows this, as does their insight, based on the dramas of the twentieth century, of the *spiritual link between those who hear and proclaim the Good News and the Jewish people* – a historical conditioning of those who receive *and* of their work of interpretation, which at the same time touches the very heart of revelation.

In the final analysis the originality of the texts of Vatican II stems from the link between two textual levels: this is precisely what I wanted to show. *On the first level, they regulate the pastoral or kerygmatic process*, such as I have outlined in its essential structure. But as soon as the ecumenical and historical-cultural implications of this act of 'handing on' in the contemporary world appear, reception comes face to face with the hermeneutical problem and with the difficulty the Fathers experienced in producing a unified formulation of the act that can not only integrate the ensemble of its parameters but also leave its mark on the treatment of all the other questions put to the Council: this is the point at which the incomplete and provisional nature of its work becomes apparent.

On the second level, the conciliar texts are therefore the expression of a gigantic process of individual and collective learning, of a sort of coming home for church consciousness at grips with modernity and other spiritual and religious forces, of a genuine 'reform' or 'conversion', incomplete, for sure, but rooted in God's Good News itself. We can follow sociologists in seeing this route taken by the Council as an 'inner secularization' of Catholicism – but on condition of not overlooking its evangelical or theologal motivations, which imply a veritable decentralization of the 'Church Group'. There is nothing to say this process, merely sketched out in December 1965, should then come to an end. On the contrary: capacity for learning or for reform is, in itself, something of the first rank and something that awaits our reception of it. So we need to see how the pastoral and ecumenical principle (first level) can integrate new outlooks, and how it can do so in response to *its own* theologal and historical requirements, which will define themselves in the process (second level). That is what, to bring my arguments to a close, I shall now risk undertaking.

III. Reception and learning

It seems to me that the forty years that separate us from the Council have in effect clarified and 're-set' at least three basic aspects of the 'inner' principle of interpretation I have just discussed: (1) the identity of Jesus of Nazareth as foundational to the Church's pastoral approach; (2) the situation of a Church in diaspora, awaiting creativity on the level of that of the early Church; (3) the cultural and religious pluralism of our societies, which leads us to rethink the eschatological status of God's Good News.

(1) Perceptive readers of the council texts may well be astonished at the little attention paid to the *Vita Christi* in this whole great body of work. Apart from brief 'summaries' in *Lumen gentium* 5 or *Dei Verbum* 2 and 4, the course of Jesus' life largely disappears behind his christological titles. There is one notable exception: the account in the Declaration on Religious Freedom (DH 11) that sets out the *modus agendi Christi*. Today, at least in the West, it is impossible not to be aware of research into the 'historical Jesus' and what is called the 'third quest', which is uncovering the Galilean's way of life in his social and cultural setting.

These researches, of which the wider public is well aware, have a double impact on the pastoral principle and its reception by the Council. In the first place, and with a totally new intensity, this is the point at which *the Jewishness of Jesus* comes up, and with it the subsequent relationship that Christian tradition bears to this through *its own* Old Testament. The return of church consciousness of the history of anti-Semitism, initiated under John Paul II, leads research back to the underlying reason for the separation between the two communities and an interrogation into the Christian approach to healing this wound. The other aspect of this 're-setting' is a more material view of Jesus' pastoral *ministry* in Galilee, viewed in *Lumen gentium* through the relatively abstract prism of the three 'functions' – priestly, prophetic, and kingly. Today we need to ask just how far the Church's universal ministry, founded on the presence of the risen Christ, is still marked by the way Jesus himself acted, as the gospel accounts convey this to us.

(2) Just after the Council, Karl Rahner drew attention to a passage, hidden in *Lumen gentium* 26, that shifts the almost unilaterally 'universalist' outlook of the Constitution toward local Churches: 'In these communities, though frequently small and poor, or living far from any other, Christ is present' (26b).[40] Rahner then in a way turns the order of reading *Lumen gentium* upside down and decodes the teaching of this text, based on the most modest and most typical local situation. Today we should undoubtedly need

to add that a far from negligible part of Western Europe is living in a spiritual situation that can no longer be interpreted in terms of 'de-Christianization'. The Decree on the Missionary Activity of the Church, *Ad gentes*, devoted to the *missio ad extra*, already cited above in a hermeneutical context, here acquires an unexpected current relevance, especially on account of its 'genetic' approach, which, in a sort of *foundation narrative*, retraces the birth of the Church on the basis of the parable of the sower (see AG 22 in particular).

The question of the *missionary creativity of the Church and the apostolic normativeness to which it is tied* is then posed in quite new terms. The debate on 'The Transmission of Divine Revelation' (DV, chapter 2) had led the Commission to reject some demands to speak of the historical founding of the Church, referring back to chapter 3 of *Lumen gentium*. This procedure, while quite legitimate in itself, supposes that the questions raised on the apostolicity of the Church, the functions of the apostles and the apostolic succession, the plurality of ecclesiologies (see Eph. 4.11–13!), the role of the Spirit, and so on, would be resolved at this point, which was not necessarily the case. The overall image of the founding of the Church that neo-scholasticism had created – a sort of a-historical, not to say ideological projection of the Church's current hierarchical structure and doctrinal architecture back into an immemorial past – has become progressively less tenable. Today we undoubtedly need to mobilize the collaboration of several disciplines – exegesis, history, systematic theology, and liturgical and pastoral theology – in order to tackle this question (which has considerable ecumenical implications) of the face of a Church that the presence of the gospel in our post-modern cultures can show today.

(3) During its last session, the Council came to shift the moral obligation of adhering to Catholicism toward the 'duty, and therefore the right, to seek the truth', though this must be done 'with prudence' (DG 3). There is no guarantee that this way of taking the autonomy of societies seriously suffices for considering the situation of radical pluralism and multi-culturalism in which we live today. The only way to justify the *eschatological status* of God's Good News while upholding the free play of communication would seem to be by arguing, reasonably and in terms that can apply universally, in favour of the capacity of *all* human being to open themselves freely to what appears to be absolute *in themselves as in others* and to experience this possibility as humanizing. By distancing itself from the '*preambula fidei*' of neo-scholastic apologetics, Vatican II had struggled against a purely extrinsicist conception of truth and had tried to take the cultural and historical rootedness of truth seriously. But in a world where every absolute religious position risks

degenerating into violence and where reason itself is threatened with madness, it has become urgent to develop an 'argument of credibility' that allows us to place them, one in relation to the other, in a position of critical articulation and thereby keep open everyone's freedom to receive an absolute Word.

*

The purpose of these few concluding remarks has been to show that the pastoral principle of Vatican II called not just for a simple application but for a real learning process, even for a capacity to envisage the *transformations* (some of which have been indicated here) produced at the heart of the constitutive interplay between those who proclaim the Good News and those who receive it, and to allow them to reflect the whole apparatus back on each other, thereby steering it toward a new 'doctrinal' balance. The normativenes of the Council texts would then consist not in their theological or juridical literalness, nor in a spirit that sees nothing more to be gained from them; *it would rather appear concretely* in pastoral or missionary applications that – guided by the Spirit – go right to the point where fresh formulations of such and such a text become evidently necessary . . . thereby awakening expectations of a new council.

Translated by Paul Burns

Notes

1. For further clarifications, see the dossier 'Une Eglise en concile: entre histoire et théologie', *RSR* 93/2 (2005). My contribution 'Pour une théologie de l'institution conciliaire' (pp. 267–90) enlarges on the hermeneutical approach selected here.
2. See above all the five volumes of Giuseppe Alberigo (gen. ed.), *Histoire du concile Vatican II. 1959–1965*, French ed., Paris and Louvain, 1997–2005.
3. Eng. trans. in W. M. Abbott (gen. ed.) *The Documents of Vatican II*, New York, London, Dublin 1966), p. 715: '. . . the authentic doctrine [. . .] should be studied and expounded through the methods of research and through the literary forms of *modern thought*. The substance of the ancient doctrine of the deposit of faith is one thing, and the way in which it is presented is another. And it is the latter that must be taken into great consideration with patience if necessary, everything being measured in the forms and proportions of a *magisterium which is predominantly pastoral in character*' (author's italics).
4. *Acta synodalia sacrosancti concili oecumenici Vaticani II* (=AS), I/4, pp. 222–27.

5. AS I/4, p. 291f.
6. AS I/4, p. 292.
7. The text has been published in G. Alberigo (ed.), *Il Vaticano II fra atteste et celebrazione*, Bologna 1995, pp. 219–24.
8. AS IV/1, p. 341.
9. The conciliar texts, in both French and English versions, are organized into the three juridical categories of Constitutions, Decrees, and Declarations. The Dogmatic Constitutions *Lumen gentium* and *Dei Verbum* open the first series, followed by the Constitution *Sacrosanctum concilium*, then the Pastoral Constiution *Gaudium et spes*.
10. French text in Jean XXIII/Paul VI, *Discours au concile*, Paris 1966, p. 107.
11. For a more detailed analysis of the structure of the *corpus*, cf. my introduction to *Vatican II. L'intégrale. Edition bilingue révisée*, Paris 2002, IV-XIII.
12. 'Vingt ans d'herméneutique du Concile', in G. Alberigo and J.-P. Jossua (eds.), *La réception de Vatican II*, Cogitatio fidei 134, Paris 1985, pp. 43–64; W. Kasper, *La théologie et l'Eglise* (1987), Cogitatio fidei 158, Paris 1990, pp. 411–23.
13. 'Vingt ans d'herméneutique', p. 51f.
14. 'Synthèse des travaux de l'assemblée synodale. Rapport final', *Documentation Catholique* (=DC) 83 (1986), p. 39.
15. Joseph Cardinal Ratzinger, 'L'ecclésiologie de la Constitution conciliaire *Lumen gentium*', DC 97 (2000), p. 304.
16. John Paul II's encyclical *Fides et ratio* (1998) could be re-read from this point of view.
17. Cf. especially Alberto Melloni (ed.), *'Movimenti' in the Church*, Concilium 2003/3.
18. Cf. in particular Congregation for the Doctrine of the Faith, 'Formules de profession de foi et du serment de fidélité', DC 86 (1989), p. 378ff; *ibid.* 'La vocation ecclésiale du théologien', DC 87 (1990), pp. 693–701.
19. *Novo millennio ineunte* (6 Jan. 2001), 57.
20. *Tertio millennio adveniente*, 20.
21. *Novo millennio ineunte*, 17–29.
22. See note 3 above.
23. In the *Generalia* of the *Disquisitio* four points are mentioned: the length of the schema, the lack of pastoral style, the lack of an ecumenical spirit, and the lack of any theological grounding for the assertions made in the text (cf. Istituto per le scienze religiose, Fonds FMGR 4. 6. 16).
24. Cf. *ibid.*
25. AS I/4, p. 388.
26. See note 19 above.
27. There are two recent studies that show a new interest in the question: Philippe Bordeyne, 'L'usage de l'Ecriture Sainte en *Gaudium et spes*. Un accès au discernement théologique et moral de la Constitution pastorale du Concile Vatican II', *Revue d'éthique et de théologie morale* 219 (Dec. 2001), pp. 67–107; Laurent

Villemin, 'Les Actes des Apôtres dans l'ecclésiologie de Vatican II', in ACFEB, *Les Actes des Apôtres. Histoire, récit, théologie*, Lectio divina 199, Paris 2005.
28. Cf. C. Theobald, 'La Révélation. Quarante ans après *Dei Verbum*', *Revue théologique de Louvain* 36 (2005), pp. 145–65.
29. AS II/5, p. 689.
30. This term was challenged by four Fathers who wanted to replace it with *renovatio* (cf. AS III/7, p. 414, n. 6).
31. Note that the text, proposed on 23 September 1964 to the assembly for revision, still refers to the *Latin version*, corrected by the Curia, of John XXIII's speech, which distinguishes between 'the deposit of faith itself, *that is the truths contained in our ancient doctrine*' and 'the form in which these truths [plural] are proclaimed'. This note disappeared from the final text, giving way once more to the *original version* of Pope John XXIII's intervention, quoted in the body of no. 6, which – at a certain remove from Vatican I – simply underlines the fundamental difference between the deposit of faith, taken here as a *whole* – without reference to an internal plurality inherent in the expression – and the historical form it takes at one time or another.
32. Cf. nonetheless certain *modi* emanating from the minority: 'The distinction between deposit of faith and manner of proclaiming the faith is considered dangerous without further explanation (111 Fathers)' (AS III/7, p. 414, n. 7).
33. In the final-but-one version the previous formulation, saying that the scriptures are capable of 'guiding and *judging* all church preaching, indeed the *Christian religion itself*' disappeared. It was finally partially re-inserted: 'All church preaching must then [. . .] be nourished and regulated [*regatur*] by Sacred Scripture.' On this point see the criticism of the text of the Constitution by Joseph Ratzinger, in his commentary on *Dei Verbum* in LThK, *Das zweite Vatikanische Konzil, II*, Freiburg 1967, pp. 519, 525.
34. AS III/1, pp 191, 207 (*relatio*).
35. Cf. AS IV/7, p. 461 (a single Father proposed the formulation that was virtually adopted).
36. AS IV/7, p. 268.
37. The first version of this passage was put forward on 7 October 1965 (AS IV/3, p. 677f); the *relatio* (AS IV/3, p. 703f) establishes a link between this section and the *aggiornamento* proposed by John XXIII.
38. The numerous corrections proposed but not accepted are a good indication of the complexity of this section.
39. See also *Dei Verbum* 12 and 13.
40. Cf. Karl Rahner, 'Das neue Bild der Kirche', in *Schriften zur Theologie VIII*, Einsiedeln 1967, pp. 329–54; 'Über die Gegenwart Christi in der Diasporagemeinde nach der Lehre des Zweiten Vatikanischen Konzils', in *ibid.*, pp. 409–25.

Is the Second Vatican Council Forgotten?

HANS KÜNG

Is the Second Vatican Council forgotten?

Around the dinner table in my childhood home in Sursee/ Switzerland, there was always talk of politics. From time to time my parents would discuss the First World War. For us as children these events were some thirty, forty years in the past. Yet all these conversations and images left us children with little more than a very vague and diffuse impression of these major events of world history. What we were lacking was having experienced them ourselves.

My thoughts often go back to this these days when I speak about the world historical events of the Second Vatican Council (1962 – 1965). For us today these are forty years in the past and as a consequence almost half the population only knows about them from hearsay or from pictures. Not least for this reason did I recount the dramatic and complex history of this Council in my *Memoir*, as I had been there myself and had made my own small contribution to it. Hence I may be permitted to dispense with the task to report on the events themselves, to offer my own impressions, scattered with anecdotes and characterizations of popes and certain bishops and theologians. In this contribution I may concentrate on what is essential under the two key terms 'legacy' and 'agenda'.

1. Legacy

Legacy: in its constitutions and decrees, decisions and impulses the Council has left us with a precious but nevertheless problematic legacy. It is a legacy which one could, instead of taking it up or making it bear fruit, reject or at least leave unused. However, how much poorer would the Catholic Church and Christianity in general be without this Council! No other Church since the Reformation has undergone a reform of this kind – in an orderly fashion and without a major schism:

1) Without the Council, the Catholic Church would still regard *religious liberty* and *tolerance* as dangerous products of the modern Zeitgeist and

Catholic countries would still deny other ('heretical') religious bodies the right to practice their faith.

After long and hard debates the Second Vatican Council took a turn which representatives of the ideology of infallibility find hard to accept: all human beings have the right to religious liberty. They are entitled particularly in matters of religion to act unhindered by oppression and according to their conscience. All religious communities have the right to practice their religion publicly, without restriction and following their own laws.

Indeed: the Second Vatican Council did on the whole terminate the discrimination of Protestants in Catholic countries. There are no more restrictions with regard to the training of pastors, the erection of church buildings, the distribution of Bibles and participation in public life. And of course, those Catholics who live in predominantly Protestant regions have also benefited from the realization of such religious freedom.

2) Without this Council, the Catholic Church would still close itself off from the *ecumenical movement* and it would still fight cold wars both on paper and in heated discussions. There would still be polemical dissociation, even militant separation in theology and society – all of it of course entirely mutual!

Vatican II did, by the skin of its teeth, recognize its share of the responsibility for the schism and the need for ongoing reform: no longer a simple 'return' of the others to an unchanged and static Catholic Church but renewal of our own Church in its life and teaching on the basis of the gospel as the prerogative for a desirable reunification. Other Christians are addressed as ecclesial communities or churches. The Council went without new dogmas and condemnations, at the explicit instruction of Pope John XXIII.

Indeed, since Vatican II the Catholic Church has to a large extent adopted an ecumenical attitude. On all levels mutual encounters, dialogue and cooperation have begun, even joint prayers and increasing fellowship in public worship. There is ecumenical convergence even in theology: it is particularly visible in biblical exegesis, in church history, religious education and practical theology, but obvious also in dogmatic theology. Therefore one could ask why in Germany in the name of ecumenism and in the light of increasing cuts in public funding one does not advance the integration of theology departments in universities (as in the USA). Here in Tübingen we were further advanced immediately after the Council than we are now. But also the relationship between congregations and especially their priests and pastors has significantly improved under the influence of Vatican II and also that of the World Council of Churches. In many cases it has become one of colleagueship or even friendship.

3) Without this Council, the Church would still regard *other world faiths* as mainly the object of negative-polemical conflict and conquistadorial missionary strategies. There would still be enmity mainly with Islam and particularly with Judaism. The racially motivated antisemitism of the National Socialists would indeed not have been ossible without centuries of anti-Judaism on the part of the Christian churches. For Vatican II however all nations with their different religions form one community: in their different ways they all seek to answer the same profound questions about the meaning and the way of life. We must therefore disregard nothing which in other faiths is perceived to be true and sacred – rays of the one truth which illuminates all of humanity. Words of high regard for Hinduism, Buddhism and especially for the followers of Islam who – following the example of Abraham – together with Christians worship the One God and honour Jesus as the prophet of God. Enmity between Christians and Muslims should be replaced by mutual understanding and shared commitment to social justice, peace and liberty. In a unique way however the Christian Church is related to the Jewish religion from which it originated and whose sacred scriptures are also hers. For the first time in history the Council rejected the idea of the 'collective responsibility' of the past or even the present Jewish people for the death of Jesus. The Council takes a stand against any idea of the ancient people of God being rejected or even under a curse, it 'decries hatred, persecutions, displays of anti-Semitism, directed against Jews at any time and by anyone' and at the same time promises to 'foster and recommend mutual understanding and respect' (*Nostra aetate*, article 4),

It cannot be overlooked: since Vatican II there has been a tremendous increase in the knowledge and respect of other faiths and especially of Judaism – in preaching, catechesis, study and conversation. Discrimination of any kind for reasons of race, skin colour, class or religion is now frowned upon. One proclaims love among all human beings as brothers and sisters under the One God. Also the possibility of salvation for non-Christians, even of well-meaning atheists, i.e. those who follow their conscience is explicitly recognized.

4) Without the Council, Catholic *liturgy* would still be a prerogative of the clergy, celebrated in a language incomprehensible to the people who are merely in attendance, in Latin High Masses and private masses whispered against a wall.

Vatican II restored the celebration of the Eucharist to be once again the worship of the whole priestly people: accessible shape, active participation of all in shared praying, singing and receiving communion. All of these are welcome realizations of the concerns of the Reformers: the medieval private

Is the Second Vatican Council Forgotten?

mass was replace by a shared public celebration; the laity was once again given the chalice, at least under certain circumstances; the introduction of the vernacular and thus the adaptation of the liturgy to different nations, finally simplification and concentration on the essence of the rite.

5) Without the Council, the Catholic Church would still neglect the theology and spirituality of the *Bible* in its preaching, academic theology and the personal piety of its members. In practical terms the Tradition of the Church is with regard to both theory and praxis above Scripture and its teaching office is above both. Biblical renewal like that of the liturgy encountered a large number of difficulties. Against modern methods of exegesis there was much opposition.

Vatican II did, though unfortunately without clearly defining the relationship between Scripture and Tradition, recognize the preeminent significance of the Bible. Within the Church all proclamation, preaching, catechesis and indeed all aspects of Christian life must be fed and guided by Scripture. The teaching office is not above the Word of God but subservient to it. The historical-critical study of the Bible was encouraged. The study of Scripture should at likewise be the soul of theology.

Indeed since Vatican II the justification of genuine historical-critical exegesis is no longer disputed and, with a very small number of exceptions, hardly impeded. The so-called inerrancy of Scripture is only claimed for the fundamental truth of salvation but not for purely scientific-historical statements. Access to Scripture for all believers has been made easier through good and partly ecumenical translations. In public worship there are readings of Scripture which are accessible and follow a new varied order of pericopes. There is now no Sunday Mass without a homily. The liturgy of the Word, even without the celebration of the Eucharist, has been restored, sometimes even led by lay people.

6) Without the Council, the *Church* would still be understood as a supernatural 'Imperium Romanum': at the top the Pope as an absolute monarch, below the 'aristocracy' of the bishops and priests, finally in a passive function the faithful people as 'subjects'. Altogether a clericalist, legalistic and triumphalist model of the Church.

Vatican II criticizes such a model of the Church and sees the Church – although with fatal compromises between medieval and biblical models of the Church – once again fundamentally not as a hierarchical pyramid but as a community of faith, as *communio*, as the pilgrim people of God, always on its way in the world. The Church is a pilgrim people which, in its sinfulness and contingency, has to be open to ongoing reform. Those who hold office within it are not above but part of the people of God, they are not its rulers but its servants. The common priesthood of all believers is to be held in high regard.

It is indeed true that since Vatican II the local churches are once again taken seriously in the context of the Church as a whole. As worshipping communities they are Church in the genuine sense of the word. The bishops shall, irrespective of the primacy of the Pope, be collectively and collegially responsible for the leadership of the universal Church – for that the Synod of Bishops was installed. Everywhere there are now diocesan and parish councils consisting of both clergy and members of the laity. Moreover even outside the Catholic Church churches and ecclesial communities are now recognized: the Council rejected the idea of the Church of Christ being the visible Catholic Church.

7) Without the Council, the *secular world* would still be viewed in largely negative terms: even in the twentieth century the Catholic Church, having lost its medieval claim to govern the world as a whole since the Reformation and the Enlightenment, liked to regard itself as a bulwark under siege. Defensively and offensively it sought to secure its traditional rights, in a rather unpleasant manner, even frequently rejecting the scientific, cultural, economic and political progress of humanity in the modern world.

Also with regard to the secular world Vatican II took a turn to the positive. The Church now seeks to be in solidarity with humanity as a whole, it will no longer reject its questions but seek to answer them. Instead of polemic there is now dialogue, instead of conquest witness.

No doubt: since Vatican II the Catholic Church has taken up many of the concerns of the Enlightenment. Today it clearly advocates the dignity, liberty and rights of humanity, for the development and improvement of human society and its institutions, for a healthy dynamic of all human creativity. Proofs for this are: an unrestricted rejection of war, advocacy of democracy and the benign separation of Church and State, cooperation in the international commonwealth of nations, emphasis on love and partnership, on personal responsibility in marriage, contemporary sexual morality ...

A contemporary sexual morality – in Rome? Here at the latest readers will want to interject: contemporary sexual morality – and what about the encyclical *Humanae Vitae* against birth control? Is that also part of the legacy of Vatican II? Unfortunately I have to tell you: yes and no. While it is not one of the Council's documents as such, it is however one of its burdens of guilt! It is founded on one of its countless fatal compromises between the overwhelming reform-minded majority and a tiny curial party in charge of the apparatus of commissions and the general secretariat of the Council.

Thus I can no longer conceal that along with its many benefits the legacy of the Council also includes burdens of guilt: compromises, dark corners, omissions, partialities, errors – a legacy that has been a tremendous burden for us all during the past four decades.

II. Agenda

Of course, we the overwhelming majority of bishops and theologians minded towards reform hoped in 1965 that to those questions which the Council had put to one side, postponed, concealed or prohibited there could be a positive response after the Council from the Pope, the Synod of Bishops or Conferences of Bishops. However, it is well known: the reform-minded majority along with the Synod of Bishops, after the Council demoted to an ineffective consultant agency, was counteracted by a curial apparatus, not in favour of reform and not in favour of the Council all along. The latter constantly attempted to impede the work of the Council and afterwards refused to take up its commission. With increasing insolence it blocked its reforms with reactionary encyclicals and declarations and mainly through strategic appointments to senior posts; only those who had passed Rome's security test could become bishops and cardinals. The longer we look at it the clearer it becomes: the Council had managed to shake up the eleventh-century Roman system of absolute power, clericalism and celibatism, but had not been able to abolish it. Rather the curial bureaucracy made every effort to restore this system *urbi et orbi*, although it was the central impediment to reconciliation with the Orthodox Churches of the East and the Reformed Churches of the West.

Although the curia had not formally rejected the legacy of the Council in the manner of the Catholic traditionalists under Archbishop Lefebvre, it had left its legacy largely lying fallow and also partly let it slip. Those conservative passages in the documents of the Council which the Curia had wrung out of it became its basic principles. Everything was interpreted staunchly backwards and the decisive aspects of progressive epochal new approaches were passed over. In spite of the demands of the Council the findings of exegesis (and the history of dogma) were not taken up, rather the tedious neo-scholastic theology was reproduced over and over again and the *Codex Iuris Canonici* was rehashed in an authoritarian fashion.

And yet with good will and a bit more theological expertise it would have been easy to achieve a solution to the outstanding problems. In my own resume of the Council, already published in 1965 and sent to Pope Paul VI, I did, alongside pointing out the positive results of the Council, draw attention to the impending *dangers* of the post-conciliar era: a crisis of a merely external authority, tensions between the Church and the Curia, the endangering of the liberty of theology, the difficulties with regard to the interpretation of the ambiguous formulations of the Council, the stagnation of post-Vatican II Catholicism, especially with regard to Canon Law. At the same time I listed eight questions which the Council had left unresolved. I will return to these below. However, in a friendly confidential letter the Pope responded as follows: 'Is it not justified to ask if the Church is served by unreserved questions which touch on the external and internal existence of the Church and its future, and this in a manner which here and there leaves necessary responsible consideration to be desired?' Thus Papa Montini.

But did not the Council commission the Church – and this is my second point – courageously to implement the resolutions of reform? Not to stop its renewal, but to act on it, in the sense of the *ecclesia semper reformanda*? Under Paul VI this did, at least to a limited extent, happen, mainly in the area of liturgical reform and with regard to ecumenical dialogue. With regard to three of the eight matters of reform raised with the Pope there was during his Pontificate significant progress: with regard to the question of mixed marriages concerning the validity of marriage and the raising of children, with regard to the praxis of penance, auricular confession and fasting, even with regard to the however tentative reform of clerical dress and titles . . .

And the other five matters of reform? Frequently I find myself thinking: how different would the Catholic Church be placed forty years after the Council if these other five concerns, shared by many at the Council and in the Church, had been taken up positively instead of ignoring them.

How easy would it have been for Montini, Pope Paul VI, an experienced man of the Curia, with the Ecumenical Council behind him, to implement a profound *reform of the Curia*: decentralization and internationalization, not merely of different nationalities, but also of different mentalities, a 'cabinet' of reformers? Instead Papa Montini decided to modernize the Curia – in the Spirit of old-style absolutism. Not to grind the bastions of Rome, but to consolidate them: an in parts even an increase of centralization, with the result that soon the Curia would once again be as strong and high-handed as it had been before the Council.

Secondly, how easy would it have been after the Council to publish a convincing encyclical about *sexuality*, a sensible *via media* between permissive libertinism and escapist rigor. It could have corrected the fatal condemnation of any kind of birth control and at the same time called for responsibility?

What came instead, was *Humanae vitae*, the said encyclical against artificial contraception: the first case in the history of the Church where the overwhelming majority of the people and the clergy refused to obey the Pope concerning an important matter (today approximately 97% of all US Catholics between 20 and 40 years of age). And that, although in the Pope's opinion this is effectively 'infallible' teaching of the 'ordinary' magisterium of the Pope and the Bishops (Art. 25 of the Constitution of the Church), in the same way as Pope John Paul II explicitly declared his condemnation of the ordination of women to be 'infallible' teaching for time and eternity. The almost complete absence of historical-critical exegesis at the Council is visible everywhere one goes.

Thirdly, how easy would it have been to resolve the question of the *law of celibacy* which it was forbidden to discuss at the Council: as before the affirmation of the scriptural free call to remain unmarried (temporarily or permanently), still the abolition of the medieval concept of lifelong compulsory celibacy for priests which is neither scriptural nor appropriate for our time? Instead there was once again the single-handed decision of the Pope: an encyclical which affirmed the law of celibacy – against the wishes of many bishops concerning this question so pertinent for the lack of priests on the continents of Latin America and Africa. This is one of the main reasons why the numbers of candidates for the priesthood and new priests in traditionally Catholic countries like Ireland or Spain has dwindled to an all-time low and in some places almost half the parishes are vacant. In Germany, there were 360 ordinations to the priesthood in 1969, still 297 in 1989 and in 2002 only 131, with a corresponding decline in the number of theology students, even Bavaria since 1986 by about 60%. Married deacons or lay theologians with limited powers, now permitted, are not a substitute for priests.

Fourthly, how easy would it have been, to include in the *election of bishops* following ancient Catholic tradition the regional churches concerned represented by the now created Councils of Priests and Pastors, and thus to involve clergy and laity, in order to achieve the necessary acceptance for bishops in this age of democracy? Instead one stuck to the secretive curial process in which candidates were mainly selected for their conformity to Rome. The biggest scandal in the history of the modern Church, mainly though not exclusively that of the USA, the sexual abuse of children and young people by priests, was systematically covered up by bishops, 90% of whom had been appointed by Pope John Paul II, less obliged to be truthful than to be obedient to the Pope.

Fifthly and finally, how easy would it have been to transfer the *election of the Pope* from the Roman College of Cardinals to the universally representative Synod of Bishops? Instead the election of the Pope is left to the body of cardinals (which had only been responsible for this since the Middle Ages), selected for this purpose on the basis of Rome's criteria by the Pope and the Curia. It is well known that in controversial questions – such as more recently with regard to counseling on pregnancy options and intercommunion – they are more concerned with the interests of Rome's position of power than with the views of the people of the Church, 80 to 90% of which disagree with in with regard to both these questions.

Thus instead of resolving these problems they were denied or sat out with backward-looking solutions. As a consequence: forty years after Vatican II the Catholic Church finds itself in an impasse, an enormous stagnation of problems and ecclesial frustration.

As far as the future is concerned: I cannot and will not rule out Rome under a new Pontificate will not in the light of the increasing pressure of problems (such as the decline of clergy numbers, the exodus of women, lack of integration of young people, the collapse of pastoral care, sexual scandals, financial problems . . .) eventually inspired by the gospel come to a new recognition of the legacy of the Council, its great spiritual legacy, so that instead of the slogans of a new conservative-authoritarian magisterium the programmatic words of John XXIII and of the Council may once again apply, i.e.:

- once again *aggiornamento* in the spirit of the gospel instead of traditional integral 'Catholic teaching' of rigorous moral encyclicals and traditionalist catechisms;
- once again colleagiality of the Pope with the bishops instead of a tight Roman centralism which in appointments to episcopal sees and academic chairs of Catholic theology ignores the interests of the local church in favour of the obedient;
- once again *appertura* to the modern world instead of accusing of, complaining about and lamenting the supposed 'complicity' with the Zeitgeist;
- once again dialogue instead of magisterial monologues, inquisition and practical refusal of the freedom of conscience and teaching within the Church;
- once again ecumenism instead of emphasizing all things narrowly Roman Catholic: even with regard to the question of the Eucharist application of John XXIII's famous distinction between the substance of the dogma of faith and its linguistic-historical presentation, a 'hierarchy of truths', not all of which are equally important.

In any case, one thing is certain in spite of all resistance and regression: the Second Vatican Council marked even for the Roman Catholic Church the end of the Middle Ages including the Counterreformation! To be more precise: the Roman-medieval, anti-modern paradigm of the Counterreformation has had its day! Many of the concerns of the Reformation and the Enlightenment have been taken up by the Catholic Church, and the paradigm shift towards a modern-post-modern constellation, whilst being slowed down from above, is far advanced from below.

Despite all disappointments: the Council was worthwhile, its resume on the whole positive! The Church after the Council is a different one from the pre-conciliar one, no doubt about it. The big debate about the future shape of the Catholic Church and Christianity as a whole however continues.

What does the future hold? No-one knows, not even John Paul II who of course wants a John Paul III. Not even he knows if there is not perhaps a Catholic Gorbachew hiding among the cardinals. Even up to the College of Cardinals there are not a small number of those who are convinced that it is impossible to go as we have done in the last 25 years. If the Catholic Church wants to have a future in the twenty-first century as a Church and note merely as a large sect, then what we need is a John XXIV. Like John XXIII, his predecessor, he should call a truly ecumenical council, a Vatican III, which sets out to find constructive answers to those questions which Vatican II left unresolved and which leads this Church from a narrow Roman Catholicism to a genuine open catholicity.

Translated by Natalie K. Watson

Further reading
Hans Küng, *My Struggle for Freedom. A Memoir*, London and New York, Continuum, 2004, especially chapters V-IX.
Hans Küng, *The Catholic Church. A Short History*, Weidenfeld & Nicholson, 2001.

The Ignored 'Text'
On the Hermeneutics of the Second Vatican Council[1]

PETER HÜNERMANN

I. The debate about the interpretation of the Council

Already during the Second Vatican Council itself the debate about the appropriate interpretation of the texts of the Council began. Its most visible sign is the *Nota explicativa praevia* to *Lumen gentium*. The founding of the journal *Concilium* immediately after the Council and the publication of the international Catholic periodical *Communio* from 1971, almost as a counter part, mark the enormity of the conflict[2] as well as the debate about the implementation of the Council in terms of Canon Law. One focus of attention are the debates about the *Lex Ecclesiae Fundamentalis*[3] and the structures of the new Code of Canon Law. The general rules of interpretation for Vatican II, published by the Synod of Bishops in 1985[4], are a response to the different hermeneutical approaches, ranging from the traditionalist rejection of Council as such to the position of those progressive circles who demanded that for the sake of its own spirit, the Council itself should be overcome.[5] A graphic example of the continuation of this debate to the present day is the discussion between Cardinal Avery Dulles and John W. O'Malley in the periodical *America* in 2003.[6]

These debates are not merely about the clarification of theoretical questions. At the heart of the debate is the general direction of the Church. The participation of ecclesial dignitaries of the highest ranks – here we should highlight particularly Cardinal Ratzinger, now the Pope, the Cardinals De Lubac, Kasper, Lehmann and Dulles – indicates the comprehensive significance of this hermeneutical debate. At the same time the specific problems of the Second Vatican Council and its reception become clear. Without a doubt the statements of the cardinals and of numerous, even internationally renowned theologians have brought about certain clarifications. But at the same time this debate also shows that the texts of the Second Vatican

Council, in spite of the fact that they were passed with only a minimal number of votes against, are not perceived as a point of reference for a consensus of the Church as a whole but as a cause for controversy.

A not insubstantial contribution to this situation, which without a doubt has a paralyzing effect on the Church, is made by those who tend to regard a stark contrast between majority and minority at the Council as the starting point for their interpretation.[7] They characterize the texts of the Council largely as statements of compromise. Thus Pottmeyer speaks of an 'internal incoherence of the texts of Council'[8]. O'Malley describes the documents of the Council as 'committee documents, full of compromises and ambiguities'[9]. Pesch finally speaks together with Seckler even of a 'contradictory pluralism'[10] which leaves the solution to a question to a forthcoming synthesis. Numerous authors find such or similar views confirmed by Paul VI who stated in his final speech at the end of the Council that it had not been the intention of the Council to resolve all questions that had been raised. Some, so Paul VI, had been postponed for the purpose of further study which the Church should undertake, others had been presented in limited and more general expressions and had been left open for a further and deeper understanding and a multitude of 'applications'.[11] The consequences of such an interpretation the Second Vatican Council can *inter alia* be seen the view held by some cannon lawyers that the publication of the CIC of 1983 offers the basic rule for the interpretation of the Second Vatican Council, insofar as here the papal teaching office explicitly refers back to the Second Vatican Council and had offered an unambiguous interpretation of the Council which resolves the ambiguities and complexities of the conciliar text.

A certain change in the debate about the hermeneutics of the Council has happened more recently as individual theologians have taken up semiotically-based textual analyses and the interpretations corresponding with them as equipment for interpreting the text. Thus Ormund Rush makes a distinction between a 'hermeneutics of the authors', the 'hermeneutics of the text' and the 'the hermeneutics of the readers'.[12] Under 'hermeneutics of the authors' he summarizes the predominant form of interpretation. In the context of a 'hermeneutics of the text' he distinguishes between the genre of the documents of Vatican II and the preceding conciliar teaching documents. The purpose of the Council was not the rejection of specific errors, for example in the form of Canones, but rather its pastoral intention to 'renew the Church in the light of pressing questions of our time'.[13] He identifies as further characteristics the rhetorical and stylistic features of the texts, their structure and the intra- and intertextuality of different texts. Only such a show of the peculiarities of the text indicates the 'spirit' of the Council which must lead the interpretation.

Rush then makes a distinction between the 'hermeneutic of the text' and the 'hermeneutic of the readers'. His starting point is Ratzinger's statement that, although the formulations of the Council's declarations are binding, their historic meaning will only unfold in the process of reception, that process of interpretation and clarification which the texts find in the life of the Church.[14] In this context Rush discusses the concept of the 'active reader' as used in modern literary criticism.[15] Thus his reflection leads to a plea for the significance of reception through the *sensus fidei* of the believers in the individual local churches with their respective cultures, their social differences etc. This is followed by a rejection of different ways of thinking about historical continuity[16] and a plea for a 'pneumatology of reception' which expects 'micro-breaks' in the stream of Tradition. Rush sees the key to this way of handling the Council and its interpretation in its own spirit in the opening sentence of *Sacrosanctum Concilium* 14:

> Mother Church earnestly desires that all the faithful should be led to that fully conscious, and active participation in liturgical celebrations which is demanded by the very nature of the liturgy. Such participation by the Christian people as "a chosen race, a royal priesthood, a holy nation, a redeemed people" (1 Pet. 2.9; cf. 2.4–5), is their right and duty by reason of their baptism.

The meaning of this sentence would have to be extended from its limiting reference to the liturgy to the ecclesial life of faith as a whole.[17]

The summary of the debate about the interpretation of Vatican II hitherto offered by Ormond Rush and the way in which he has enriched this debate through the integration of moments of textual hermeneutics and hermeneutics of the reader is highly commendable. There is however at the end the pointed question: in order to get to the way of dealing with Tradition and the Tradition of faith in particular, do we need the Second Vatican Council? Do we need to study its texts to come to this conclusion? Are these not general perspectives of a kind which no longer require the texts of Vatican II and the Council's struggle for particular formulations?[18] Does this not mean that the Council rather loses its function of orientation?

In addition to this there are factual concerns related to the interrelationship of the three hermeneutics to which the author refers: the hermeneutics of the author, of the text and of the reader. In this outline they seem to stand next to each other without being interwoven with each other.

In order to make some progress with regard to this rather complex question of an appropriate interpretation of the Second Vatican Council I want, following the distinction between a hermeneutics of the 'authors', the 'text' and the 'readers', to raise central question which has so far not been raised in this debate, the question about the genre of the documents of the Council. From there we can then move in further steps to approach the text itself.

II. A central question ignored

Rush summarizes authors under the term 'hermeneutics of the authors', and theologians who, as Ormond Rush himself, O'Malley or Gerhard Hall, start from a necessary hermeneutics of the text which includes the literary critical questions of rhetoric and style as well as from a 'hermeneutics of the reader' which complements the 'hermeneutics of the authors'. They all ignore one question. The central question which has not been dealt with by all of these exegetes is the question about the genre of the documents.[19]

The great Councils of the Church since Nicea have passed Canones, magisterial definitions and legal texts which concern the order and the life of the Church.[20] Matthias Joseph Scheeben therefore attributes – following Vatican I – the conciliar decrees formally to the *potestas jurisdictionis*.[21] The textual genres of such conciliar decrees are 'judgments' and 'laws'. Scheeben therefore refers to 'teaching prescriptions'. The texts of the Second Vatican Council do obviously not represent this genre of texts. A number of the interpreters of the Second Vatican Council as well as among those who participate in the hermeneutical discussions there are those who lament that – in contrast to other councils – there are no clear positions of doctrinal condemnation. Others talk about the fact that this Council, as it understands itself as pastoral and did not present any definitions, must be interpreted in the light of the dogmatic definitions of the preceding councils, i.e. Vatican I and Trent. What manner of a genre of text are we dealing with them? Ormond Rush states:

> The genre of the documents of Vatican II is unique in the history of conciliar teaching. Pastoral in its orientation, the Council consciously did not intend to take up specific errors but to renew the Church in the light of the urgent questions of our time.'[22]

While this statement covers what can be said in general terms about the intention of the text, it does not *name* the specific genre of text, but merely delimits it in negative terms against the judicial 'teaching prescriptions of earlier councils.

The answer given by the Council itself to the question of the binding character of the individual documents refers to the text itself.[23] It states that 'definitions' are only given where this is evident in the texts themselves, and everywhere else underlines the binding character of all its pronouncements.

Why is the question regarding the genre of the texts of the Second Vatican Council so significant? Because the exact attribution of the authors and their intention with regard to the text ensues first of all from the genre of the text. Likewise results from the genre of the text the basic manner in which readers and addressees are bound by the text and its orientation as well as its content and in which way they are to employ their creativity.

Three small examples may serve as clarification:

a) A letter – as a genre of text – largely determined by the intention of its author; s/he wants to communicate to the recipient an important message or just a friendly sign of life. Thus the intention of the text is essentially determined by the intention of the author, although a letter may also convey something about matters and concerns, which are not immediately within the author's intention, such as the cultural background of the writer etc. At the same time it is required of the reader to tie themselves primarily to this intention of the author and not for example in the case of a lyrical poem to take into account all manner of aesthetic questions and considerations. In doing so they would overstretch the text.

b) The situation is very different where a lyrical poem is concerned; the empirical intention of the author, her or his immediate intention almost entirely recedes behind the intention of the text. The text, once published, stands as it were in itself and develops its own intention in order to assess its significance the reader's aesthetic and historical potentiality is required in its entirety. This however does not mean arbitrariness, as the interpretation needs to be rooted in the text itself and in references from it which support and justify the interpretation.[24]

c) Let us look at our third genre: a law. A judge is bound by a law in a very specific way. Thus for example in the case of English Civil Law the actual text is to the fore (golden rule); the intentions of the legislator as in the earlier common law are taken into account as additional points of reference for its interpretation (mischief rule). Since the 1960s the 'purposive approach' is applied: 'the literal meaning of the words is never allowed to prevail where it would produce manifest absurdity or consequences which can never have been intended by the legislator . . .'[25] Thus we find that also in this case a certain relation between authors and readers ensues which is different in a specific way from the poetic genre of text or from the letter as text.

The Ignored 'Text'

Thus the question is irrefutable: how can the genre of text of the Second Vatican Council be defined?

III. Reflection on the genre of text of the Second Vatican Council

The following steps of reflection respectively approach the definition of the genre of text from different perspectives as one approaches an object which is only vaguely known by as it were looking at it from different angles.

a) The documents of Vatican II are a 'conciliar text'.

This statement seems to be banal, but is highly relevant.[26] A range of possible interpretations are thus ruled out. A council does not merely consist of 'empirical human beings', it does not simply express these people's opinions. A council that has been legitimately convoked – and Vatican II understands itself as such – represents the magisterium of the Church. Together with the Pope it is the highest teaching authority. It claims – even where this is not formally declared – authentically to interpret the revelation of God. Thus it is binding for all believers from the Pope to members of the laity, to individual faithful such as congregations, local churches, the Church universal and its respective institutions.

This means that with regard to the 'hermeneutics of the authors' the 'authors' intention' essentially recedes behind the 'intention of the text'. Only in the 'intention of the text' does the 'magisterium' come to the fore. Historical investigations regarding the intentions and meanings of particular texts which are connected with the names of individual Council Fathers or groups of Council Fathers are thus merely auxiliary moments for the interpretation of the text. This also applies to groups such as 'majority', 'minority' etc. Such historically identifiable particular moments must fundamentally be interpreted out of the 'intention of the text'. As a consequence one cannot read a conciliar text as a juxtaposition of different views, as the emergence of the text, the historical or empirical process of becoming acquires a new quality in its result: the text becomes a text of the Council and thereby claims to be an authentic and binding interpretation of the faith.

What follows with regard to the hermeneutics of the reader from this 'banal' thesis is that the text wants to say to the reader something which is binding in all its sections and chapters. Thereby all 'selective hermeneutics' is ruled out. The text itself prescribes orientations which are binding for the 'hermeneutics of the reader' and prohibit any form of unruly and inappropriate 'creativity'. Together with the conclusion that the documents of

Vatican II are a 'conciliar text', all general rules are given, which for example Walter Kasper highlights in his contribution to hermeneutics of the Council[27]: interpretation in the context of Scripture and Tradition as a whole etc.

b) Vatican II is a peculiar council

The general statements made under a) gain a sharpened sense through the peculiar character of Vatican II. This peculiar character is highlighted in comparing it to Trent and the First Vatican Council.

The Council of Trent issued magisterial definitions and reform decrees in the light of the bad state of affairs within the Church and the doctrinal theses of the Reformation. Through conciliar work the Council triggered a history of interpretation which led to a considerable renewal in all parts of Church life.

In a similar fashion Vatican I responded with definitions to the unconditional claims of modern science and the claims of absolute sovereignty of modern states.[28] This Council too triggered a wide history of interpretation. The Church acquired a different face. One expression of this is – alongside many other moments – the reshaping of Canon Law.

Vatican II joins this tradition, albeit with the decisive difference that this Council does not see itself to be compelled to undertake defining condemnations. It rather aims for the kind of renewal of the Church and its life which emerged following Trent and Vatican I as history of interpretation. This peculiarity of the Second Vatican Council also ensues from the Council being called by John XXIII[29] as in the decisions of the Council Fathers, mainly during the first Session[30], the way of working developed by them[31], the important statements by Paul VI about the purpose and work of the Council.[32]

c) Approximation to the specific genre of text – a classification of qualities

While in part b) we found ourselves largely in agreement with Ormond Rush, the next and the following steps will take us beyond him.

It is clear that the specific characteristic of the genre of text and the peculiarity of the Council are a unit. While what is proper to the Council, as it finds expression in its convocation, its ways of working and the decisions of the Council Fathers, covers the *steps which constitute the genesis of the text*, the genre of the text is nothing but the manifestation the result of this genesis of the text: the form which fundamentally gives identity to the corpus of the documents of the Council. Let us approach the classification of the genre of the texts by using what is proper to the Council in its manifold manifestations as orientation.

The genre of the text is shaped by a *fundamental reflection*. Paul VI summarized the agenda of the Council, as prescribed by John XXIII and taken up and realized by the Council itself, in the question: 'Church, what say ye about thyself?' The documents of the Council are a fundamental reflection on what the Church in the modern world is, what it is supposed to do, how it presents itself in relation to humanity, to the religions and to the developments of modernity. Fundamental reflection in this context means theological reflection which is however not undertaken in order further to clarify matters of the doctrine of God, of Christology, of Pneumatology etc. It is a theological reflection which is meant to illuminate the fundamental orientation of the Church in its historic existence. Accordingly for example the constitution on revelation begins with a reflection on the God who reveals himself, speaks of revelation in the economy of salvation in the Old Testament and characterizes Jesus Christ, his life and witness, his death, his resurrection and the sending out of his disciples, in order to characterize from there the presence of the divine revelation and its passing on through Scripture and Tradition, going from there on to the basic principles of exegesis and the role of meditation on Scripture in the faith lives of individuals and congregations.[33] As this is a fundamental theological reflection with regard to the Church and the ecclesial lives of the faithful, the foundational questions are of necessity discussed on different levels. The different levels have their respective material logic. They must however be seen in relation to homology. At the same time there is a respective context of foundation.[34]

The genre of the text presents the *principles* of the life and social order of the Church. The fundamental theological reflection referred to in the previous section is structured in a way that through being broken up the different levels the principles of the life and social order of the Church become visible. Fundamental theological reflection can take place against different horizons and with a variety of emphases. The texts of the Second Vatican Council are concerned with working out those *principles* which enable, carry and define the lives of the faithful and the shared life within the Church, with humanity and the world. This characteristic too is very visible in the great debate which led to the abandonment of the pre-prepared scheme about the relationship between Scripture and Tradition and led to the complete re-development of the scheme on revelation. The intensity with which the Council Fathers point out that one cannot speak to today's people as the pre-prepared scheme had proposed is striking. Time and time again one finds general references to the lack of pastoral character in these statements.[35]

The genre of the text of the Second Vatican Council is characterized by its claim to be the *measure* of all ecclesial activities. As the principles name those roots out of which faithful living and ecclesial being together are fed, out of which her living development and being together can grow, the concept of 'measure' presents the normative character connected with the principles. This means that the corpus of the Council texts does not merely depict ecclesial reality. Neither does it however draw up an ideal without taking care that it is of necessity 'earthed'. The documents represent a genre which contains norms for different levels. This means that these norms do not merely take place on the juridical level, they also refer to the levels of ethics and social ethics as well as to the praxis of faith, hope and live, of piety of the individual and corporate kind. They are operationable norms. In doing this the Council by no means claims encyclopedic completeness. It wants to work out fundamental orientations of a normative kind, and the Council Fathers frequently refer back to typical situations and fundamental model answers. This 'combination' corresponds to the fundamental theological reflection outlined about and the carving out of the principles of the life and social order of the Church.

The genre of the text is determined by the fact that the documents of the Second Vatican Council present themselves as the *fundamental consensus* of the Catholic Church.

The *fundamental consensus* incorporates a wealth of reference points. The text claims on the one hand the identity of the faith as it is, witnessed to be Scripture and Tradition, to be interpreted in our time. This implies therefore assent, agreement to the decisive testimonies of revelation and the tradition of the events of revelation, as well as the taking into account of the present situation of human beings, of humanity and of the world. This fundamental consensus of faith is witnessed to by the entire College of Bishops under its head the Pope, gathered in the Council. The text furthermore claims to represent the consensus of the different local churches and of the universal Church, which have factually and legally received these documents, with the exception of a small group around Archbishop Lefèbvre who had entered into schism with it. As such a document of *fundamental consensus* the text likewise exercises a function of authorization and that of deciding in case of argument. At the same time it fulfills a limiting function with regard to the exercise of authority in the Church.

It is finally a genre of text which takes precedence over all other authoritative instructions and pronouncements which can be proclaimed by authorities in the Church.

By decree and being put into force the Pope and the Bishops as well as all other faithful are bound by this text. With regard to all forms of exercising authority this text is to be taken into account and to be respected. This precedence is clearly expressed for example in the Apostolic Constitution *Sacrae Disciplinae Leges* and in the Preface of the Codex Iuris Canonici of 1983. 'The reform was to be carried out according to the decisions and principles to be determined by that same Council.'[36]

How then can we name the genre of the texts of the documents of the Second Vatican Council which is characterized by the qualities outlined above?

d) The appropriate naming of the genre of the texts

Traditionally an appropriate naming of facts includes 'genus' and '*differentia specifica*'. The genre connects the relevant facts with a range of other facts which have a family similarity. The *differentia specifica* are what distinguishes the facts in question from other facts. The first question which we need to ask is therefore: where are similar texts which have the same characteristics as those outlined above?

Here we can refer to constitutional texts. Constitutional texts most often emerge out of a crisis or an essential desire for innovation on the part of a state.[37] They represent a fundamental reflection on the order of life of human beings in a state where at the same time the leading principles emerge from which the life and social order is developed. A constitution prescribes the normative framework, the measure for legal and political action but also for the activities of civil society. It is an expression of a fundamental consensus of society and legitimizes the foundational authorities whilst at the same time delimiting their functions. Finally a constitution in the context of the state is the highest form of such a fundamental order'. It is comprehensive, i.e. it extents to all citizens and the strangers in a given state, it has an effect in all areas of life and as a consequence it is not simply selective or particular.[38]

If the documents of the Council as a corpus of texts belong to the genre of constitutional texts, we also have to identify the *differentia specifica* in contrast to the constitutions of states. One aspect of the *differentia specifica* already emerges from a historical point of view: modern state constitutions develop in the light of the collapse of the power and authority of the monarchy which derived its authority from its original or divine rights. Connected with the constitution and its consensus was thus the constitution of a new highest state power. In contrast the Church at Vatican I derived the authority in the Church from divine institution. As in state constitutions however the texts of Vatican II also discuss the competences and limitations of the competences and the authority within the Church, especially with regard to the manner in which these competences are to be exercised, what kind of a spirit has to shape the institutional relationships etc.

A second fundamental difference with regard to the text of the constitution of a state is that the text of a state constitution refers to the legal-political dimension of public life, the text of the Council however to the institutional-public-legal dimension as well as to the levels of morality and ethics and questions regarding the praxis and the convictions of faith. One will as a consequence be able to describe the genre of the text of Vatican II as a 'constitution of faithful ecclesial life' or for short as 'constituant of faith'. The latter term is probably to be preferred, as it avoids the obvious misconception that it is merely a legal institutional constitution of the Church as it had been planned in the *Lex Fundamentalis Ecclesiae*.

IV. Some conclusions from the classification of the genre of the text

a) *Ambiguities and 'contradictory pluralism'*

The sharpest criticism of the text of Vatican II is probably the accusation that it is a text of compromise, one could 'in the case of the extreme not infrequently expect the compromise of 'contradictory pluralism'[39]. Constitutional lawyers state however that most constitutional texts have a fragmentary and compromise character[40]: constitutions frequently have a fragmentary character as they present fundamental reflections and approach principles without always reaching completeness, and they leave their implementation to the different competent institutions. Constitutions frequently have the character of a compromise as they outline an 'order of peace' which has to include different points of view. Concrete mediation can frequently not be achieved by the body that sets the constitution. If this applies to the genre of constitutional texts in general, it also applies to the 'constitution of faith' as presented by the Second Vatican Council.

Let us go back to Pesch's example of the third chapter of the Dogmatic Constitution on the Church *Lumen gentium* which teaches about the collegiality of the bishops and the primatial power of the Pope.[41]

The Council obviously regarded both moments, collegiality and primatial power, as essential. The Church has and requires primatial power, and she is essentially shaped by the collegiality of the episcopate as a whole.[42]

It goes without saying that the connection and the mediation of both moments requires a theological and primarily a practical mediation. The direction for the shape of the theological and practical mediation is given by the references to the Synod of Bishops in *Lumen gentium* itself[43], although the Council by no means says that the introduction of the Synod of Bishops – which by the way can take different shapes – does by no means already answer or realize the question of the mediation of both principles. The way in which Pope John Paul II takes up the question about the 'how' of the primatial power in his encyclical *Ut unum sint* points in the same direction.[44]

That the purpose and the function of primatial power are maintained, even when the day to day work of governance is largely undertaken by the Synod, if for example for grave reasons a primatial veto is possible and in extraordinary situations there is a primatial competence to act, cannot be denied.[45]

Starting from the given genre of the text we can neither see the possibility nor the necessity to speak with regard to the statements about primacy and collegiality in *Lumen gentium* about a 'contradictory pluralism'. Such a possibility only ensues if one starts out from a conciliar text which in terms of genre has the form of a law or a judgment.

b) Specific endangering and limitations of the said genre of text

Constitutions are a genre of text which in spite of its authority is in extreme danger and cannot be easily secured. *Mutatis mutandis* this also applies to the corpus of the texts of Vatican II. Constitutional texts doe not simply depict the factual 'constitution of a given society'. The real balances of power, the 'pecking orders' can differ quite significantly from the structures outlined in the text of the constitution. It goes without saying that different centres of power will time and time again seek to extend their spheres of influence. Thus the text of a constitution only remains in force as it is carried and supported by the respective general consensus. By no means all states have made provision for a constitutional court. It is certainly an important means for calling to mind the weightiness of the constitution and to remind the responsible agents of their being bound by the constitution. Yet a constitutional court is by a means an instrument of absolute security. There are plenty of constitutions in the world of states which in effect only exist on paper and have now binding power.[46]

Such a situation can begin by the constitution being 'undermined'. Such an undermining is not yet a formal breach of the constitution. Grimm describes the undermining of a constitution as follows: 'One can speak of the reality of the constitution being undermined when political institutions or practices emerge which the constitution neither permits not forbids, but which nevertheless detract from the realization of the aims set by the constitution or from the functioning of those institutions and procedures intended by the constitution.[47] A *breach* of the constitution takes place when the regulations of the constitution as such are breached, especially when such a breach becomes common practice.

The endangering and the limitations of the text genre of 'constitution' lie thus in the fact that the constitution depends on a consensus of liberty, especially that of the different authorities.

This endangering and this specific type of limitation also apply to the text corpus of Vatican II. Experiences throughout the history of the church show how susceptible even ecclesial authorities are to the temptations of power. It is self-evident that modernity presents entirely new types of the accumulation of power. On the basis of changes with regard to the possibilities of communication, the immensely intensified possibilities of organization, forms of influencing the masses and of creating centralistic forms of government and administration which had been hitherto unknown. The question emerges to what extent the premises of Vatican II can stand their ground even in a situation like this, both with their specific emphases and with the statements which seek to limit authority. Here too there are possibilities of 'undermining' and of 'breaching the constitution'. It is only possible to safeguard the text of Vatican II if the different groups, the different authorities, the People of God refer to Vatican II, if they claim and enforce its validity and normativity again and again. The work of theologians and canon lawyers will be of particular importance in this respect.

c) *The genre of text, the history of reception and the future of Vatican II*

At the conclusion of this sketch shall be a short reflection on the history of the reception and a preview on the future of Vatican II. Immediately after the Council there was a first wave of reception connected with a profound reform based on the instructions of the Council. The reform of the liturgy and the revision of the *Codex Iuris Canonici* are only the most visible signs for this. No less remarkable are the transformations in the area of theology triggered by the Council, especially in the emergence of types of theology specific to different continents and cultural contexts.[48] Of the greatest importance however are the transformations among the People of God, in the unfolding of their consciousness of having come of age, of being able to think for themselves and of their own responsibility, especially among the laity.

It cannot be ignored that in the course of the history of reception the actual balance of power within the Church came to the fore. These developments partly had the characteristics of undermining the constitution, as the justifications for such decisions and decrees use selective quotations from Vatican II as proof texts. The most recent pronouncements with regard to the liturgy cancelled out a number of conciliar instructions.[49] With regard to the future it is even more decisive than such events whether it will be possible to adopt the corpus of the texts of Vatican II as a *lasting guide line*. Its true character will only come to the fore if it is not merely regarded as fulfilling a one-off function, but if it is used time and time again for the resolution of the respective problems of different times.

This also means that even the revision of the order of life in the church as it has taken place so far – on the basis of the wave of reception – must be put to the test from time to time. It does not mean that the reception hitherto is called into question in its entirety. Yet we have to look at those areas in the life of the contemporary Church where urgent questions and problems arise, for example with regard to the centralism in the Church about which a large number of bishops and local churches complain. Forty years after the end of the Second Vatican Council the issue of this abiding critical function of the conciliar text is the decisive hermeneutical question.

Translated by Natalie K. Watson

Notes

1. More detailed analyses and justifications as well as further bibliographies can be found in the author's contribution to *Herders Theologischer Kommentar zum Zweiten Vatikanischen Konzil* (HThK Vat. II), ed. by Peter Hünermann and B.J. Hilberath, vol. 5 *Der Text – Gestalt, Werden, Bedeutung*, Freiburg 2005.
2. The heat and bitterness of the debate become apparent in Henry de Lubac's memoirs, *Meine Schriften im Rückblick*, Einsiedeln/ Freiburg, 1996, pp. 476–483.
3. W. Aymans, 'Das Project einer Lex Ecclesiae Fundamentalis' in *Handbuch des katholischen Kirchenrechts*, ed J. Listl, H. Müller and H. Schmitz, Regensburg, 1983, pp. 68ff.; Paolo La Terra, 'La formalizzazione die doveri-diritti fondamentali dei fedeli nei progretti di lex ecclesiae fundamentalis fino al codex iuris canonici del 1983', Pontificia Universitas Lateranensis, Thesis ad Lauream, Rome, 1994.
4. Cf *Zukunft aus der Kraft des Konzils. Die außerordentliche Bischofssynode '85. Die Dokumente mit einem Kommentar von W. Kasper*, Freiburg 1986, as well as *Concilium* 22/6 (1986): *Synod 1985 – an evaluation*.

5. Cf. *Die Rezeption des II. Vatikanischen Konzils* edited by Hermann Josef Pottmeyer, Giuseppe Alberigo and Jean-Pierre Jossua, Düsseldorf, 1986; see especially the article by Menozzi.
6. Cf. *America* 188 (2003), 6 (24 February), pp. 7–15; 9 (17 March), pp. 14f. 29f; 11 (31 March), pp. 11–17.
7. Cf. Antonio Acerbi, *Due ecclesiologie. Ecclesiologia giurdica ed ecclesiologia di communione nella* "Lumen gentium" (Collana nuovi saggi teologici 4), Bologna, 1975 and Max Seckler, 'Über den Kompromiss in Sachen der Lehre' in *Begegnung. Beiträge zu einer Hermeneutik des theologischen Gesprächs*, Graz/Vienna/Cologne, 1972, pp 45–57.
8. Cf. Hermann Josef Pottmeyer, 'Von einer neuen Phase der Rezeption des Vaticanum II. Zwanzig Jahre Hermeneutik des Konzils' in *Die Rezeption des II. Vatikanischen Konzils* edited by Hermann Josef Pottmeyer, Giuseppe Alberigo and Jean-Pierre Jossua, Düsseldorf, 1986, pp. 47–65.
9. John W. O'Malley, *Tradition and Transition: Historical Perspectives on Vatican II*, Theology and Life series 26, Wilmington/ Del., 1989, p. 45.
10. Cf. Seckler, *ibid*, p. 56f, footnote 7; Otto Hermann Pesch, *Das Zweite Vatikanische Konzil (1962–1965): Vorgeschichte – Verlauf – Ergebnisse – Nachgeschichte*, Würzburg, 1993, pp. 150–154.
11. Speech in the public meeting of the Second Vatican Council of 7 December 1965, cf. HThK Vat. II, vol. 5 (Supplement).
12. Cf. Ormond Rish, *Still Interpreting Vatican II. Some Hermeneutical Principles*, New York – Mahway, N.J., 2004.
13. *Ibid.*, p. 36.
14. Cf. Joseph Ratzinger, *Theologische Prinzipienlehre. Bausteine zur Fundamentaltheologie*, Munich, 1982, pp. 39f.
15. He does however not consider that the distinction between the concept of the 'ideal reader' in contrast to the empirical reader is primarily made in the context of poetic texts and their interpretation.
16. Cf. Rush, *ibid.*, pp. 58–63; 72–76; John W. O'Malley, *Tradition and Transition: Historical Perspectives on Vatican II*, Wilmington, Del, 1989, pp. 44–81 and 'The Style of Vatican II. The "how" of the Church Changed During the Council' *America* 188 (2003), 6 924 February), pp. 12–15; Joseph A. Komonchak, 'Vatican II as an "Event"' *Theology Digest* 46 (1999), pp. 337–352.
17. Cf. Rush, *ibid.*, pp. 81f/
18. These questions are particularly raised by Rush's concluding reflection where he presents some very general maxims about meaning and dealing with the documents.
19. O'Malley raises the question about the new 'genre' of the texts of Vatican II and points to their being different from those of previous councils. He demands that the rules of interpretation be extended to make this point. He does however not take the question about the genre any further but instead emphasizes the style of its language. Cf. John W. O'Malley, 'Vatican II: Official Norms. On inter-

preting the council, with a response to Cardinal Avery Dulles' *America* 188 (2003) 11 (31 March), pp. 11–14, here 14. O'Malley formulates the central question 'how did the Council teach?' How did it say what it wanted to say? Here, so Malley, the Council entered a 'new language game'. The question about the genre of the text which is raised here goes beyond such a question of the 'how'. It does not aim for the individual style but for 'typical;' forms of texts and their specific pragmatics.

20. The insertion into the Creed decided by the Council of Nicea is defined with precision by the likewise passed canon.
21. Cf. Matthias Joseph Scheeben, *Handbuch der katholischen Dogmatik* Bd. 1 *Theologische Erkenntnislehre*, Freiburg, 1959, pp. 72–80: 'The authoritative doctrinal teaching belongs as legislative resp. judicial act like those decrees which concern administration and oversight obviously not formally to the *potestas ordinis* but to the *potestas jurisdictions* resp,. to that special branch of the same which is technically described as the power of the magisterium..' (*ibid.*, p. 73, translation NKW).
22. Rush, *ibid.*, p. 36.
23. Cf. Notificatio of 15 November 1965: 'In consideration of the conciliar custom and the pastoral intention of this present Council this Holy Synod defines only those matters which concern matters of faith and custom as to be kept by the Church, which she herself has explicitly declared to be such. All other matters presented by the Holy Synod are to be accepted by all and individual believers in Christ as teaching of the highest magisterium of the Church. They cover thus those matters following the Holy Synod's own intention and are either realized as such due to their subject matter or their manner of speech, following the guidelines for theological interpretation.' As quoted in HThK Vat II., vol 1 *Die Dokumente des II. Vatikanischen Konzils*, Freiburg, 2004, p. 386. Translation: NKW.
24. Umberto Eco says about the role of readers of poetic texts: 'The reader – as the active principle of interpretation – is part of the generative framework of one and the same text.' Umberto Eco, *Lector in fabula*, Munich and Vienna, 1987, p. 8. This translation: NKW.
25. Cf. Dieter Henrich and Peter Huber, *Einführung in das englische Privatrecht*, Heidelberg, 3rd edition, 2003, pp. 29–31.
26. Cf. Peter Hünermann, 'Zu den Kategorien "Konzil" und "Konzilsentscheidung" – Vorüberlegungen zur Interpretation des II. Vatikanums' in *Das II. Vatikanum – Christlicher Glaube im Horizont globaler Modernisierung* ed. by Peter Hünermann, Programm und Wirkungsgeschichte des II. Vatikanums vol. 1, Paderborn, 1998, pp. 67–82.
27. Cf Walter Kasper, 'The Continuing Challenge of the Second Vatican Council; The Hermeneutics of the Conciliar Statements' in Walter Kasper, *Theology and Church*, translated by Margaret Kohl, London, 1989, p. 166–176.
28. Cf Hermann Josef Pottmeyer, *Unfehlbarkeit und Souveränität. Die päpstliche*

Unfehlbarkeit im System der ultramontanen Ekklesiologie des 19. Jahrhunderts, TTS 5, Mainz, 1975.

29. Cf. *inter alia* the announcement of the Council on 25 January 1959, the radio broadcast of 11 September 1962, the opening speech of the Council '*Gaudet Mater Ecclesia*'. For a critical edition of the announcement of the Council see Alberto Melloni'„Questa festiva ricorrenza". Prodromi e preparazione del discorso di annuncio del Vaticano II (25 Gennaio 1959), *Reivista di storia e letteratura religiosa* 28 (1992) pp. 607–643; for a critical edition of the opening speech: Alberto Melloni, 'Sinossi critica dell'allocuzione di apertura del Concilio Vaticano II "Gaudet Mater Ecclesia" die Giovanni XXIII' in *Fede Tradizione Profezia, Studi su Giovanni XXIII. E sul Vaticano II*, vol. 21, Brescia 1984, pp. 239–283. Further documents can be found in HThK Vat.II, vol. 5 (Supplement).

30. Particular attention should be drawn to the discussion about the prepared scheme of the dogmatic constitution regarding the sources of revelation from 14–21 November 1962; cf. Giuseppe Ruggieri, 'La discussione sullo schema constitutionis dogmaticae de fontibus revelationis durante la I sessione del Concilio Vaticano II' in *Vatican II commence ... Approches Francophones* ed. by É. Fouilloux, Leuven 1993, pp. 315–328.

31. Cf. Ruggieri, *ibid.*. Furthermore: Giuseppe Alberigo, 'Dinamiche e procedure nel Vaticano II. Verso la revisione del Regolamento del Concilio (1962–63)' in *Cristianesimo nella storia* 13 (1992), pp. 115–164.

32. Cf. the speech at the opening of the Second Session of the Council on 29 September 1963, *HThK Vat. II*, vol. 5 (Supplement).

33. Cf. HThK Vat. II, vol. 3, pp. 695–831.

34. The structure of DV is a textbook example of the sequence of these different levels beginning with the highest level of divine self communication to the concrete historic manifestations for example in dealing with Scripture. Typically enough this structure is not only found in the great constitutions. It has also come to the fore in the debates about decrees such as *Prebyterium ordinis*, which originally were nor supposed to start from a foundational theological reflection but were supposed to take up matters of the immediate praxis. Very similar the process around *Ad gentes*, the decree on mission. Cf. the commentaries on PO and AG in HThk Vat. II, vol. 4.

35. CF. Ruggieri, *ibid.*, note 30.

    Cf. also the numerous references in PO which highlight that the risen Lord, present in the Spirit, works through the service and the lives of priests and does his work through such everyday events: 'In order to continue doing the will of his Father in the world, Christ works unceasingly through the Church. He operates through his ministers . . .' PO 14,2. 'The purpose, therefore, which priests pursue in their ministry and by their life is to procure the glory of God the Father in Christ. That glory consists in this-that men working freely and with a grateful spirit receive the work of God made perfect in Christ and then manifest it in their whole lives.' PO 2,4.

Similarly for example the statements in AA2,4 and 5 about the apostolate of the laity; AA 1,2 speaks about the 'unmistakable work being done today by the Holy Spirit in making the laity ever more conscious of their own responsibility and encouraging them to serve Christ and the Church in all circumstances'. In AG 9,2 the missionary activity of the Church is characterized as follows: 'Missionary activity is nothing else and nothing less than an epiphany, or a manifesting of God's decree, and its fulfillment in the world and in world history, in the course of which God, by means of mission, manifestly works out the history of salvation. By the preaching of the word and by the celebration of the sacraments, the center and summit of which is the most holy Eucharist, He brings about the presence of Christ, the author of salvation.'

36. Code of Canon Law, Preface to the Latin edition, here quoted as found on http://www.vatican.va/archive/ENG1104/__P1.HTM.
37. Vgl. Paolo Pombeni, 'La dialettica evento-decisioni nella ricostruzione delle grandi assemblee. I parlamenti e le assemblee costituenti' in: Maria Teresa Fattori – Alberto Melloni (eds), *L'evento e le decisioni. Studi sulle dinamiche del concilio Vaticano II*, Bologna 1997, pp. 17–49.
38. The main points with regard to the characteristic of constitutional texts are taken from Dieter Grimm, 'Verfassung' *Staatslexikon*, vol. 5, Freiburg, Basle, Vienna, 7th edition 1989, pp. 633–643.
39. Otto Hermann Pesch, *Das II. Vatikanische Konzil (1962–1965)*, Würzburg, 1993, p. 151. Pesch explains the term ‚contradictory pluralism' as follows: ‚At the Second Vatican Council a kind of compromise emerged, which according to Max Seckler no ecclesial gathering had ever permitted itself. It is connected with the 'group-dynamic' processes at the Council itself. And it was made easier by the fact that the Council, contrary to the expectations of some, had consciously gone without formulating its decrees in the form of an ultimately binding dogma. The result is not only textual material which is not entirely balanced – this is rarely achieved by the work of committees of this kind of extent, also not only that there are logical leaps – that could have been avoided then and in spite of the pressure of time even now. What is decisive is that many a text could only be got through on the basis of 'if you accept my text, I will concede yours'. Somewhat maliciously – with regard to the human attitude behind it, i.e. with the wink of understanding, Seckler calls this the 'compromise of reciprocal dishonesty'. As a matter of fact one would, following Seckler, have to speak about a 'compromise of contradictory pluralism'. (*Ibid.*, p. 152f.)
40. Cf. Dieter Grimm, *ibid.*, note 39.
41. Pesch remarks: 'In the third chapter of the Constitution on the Church, where, after many debates, the doctrine of the collegiality of the bishops was supossed to be enacted, and indeed was, speaks in the final result more of the primatial power of the Pope than even the First Vatican Council. And in the 'Explanatory preliminary remark' (*nota praevia*) we even find the hitherto unheard of statement that the Pope could exercise his power at any time *ad placitum*, i.e. at his

own discretion. It is understandable that the minority, being pushed into a position of defense sought their salvation in piling up references to the Pope – and that the others conceded them to do it, as their own concerns could otherwise only be pushed through by a massive vote' (*ibid.*, p. 153).

42. The text, which the Commission had prepared, explicitly refers to both moments, primatial power and colleagiality. The *Nota explicativa praevia*, at first brought to the attention of the Commission, then 'proclaimed' by the Secretary of the Council 'in the name of a higher authority', does not in terms of content bring any new moments into play. Cf. this author's Commentary on *Lumen gentium* in HThK Vat. II, vol. 2, pp. 539–547.
43. Cf. LG 22 and HThk Vat. II, vol. 2, pp. 420–428.
44. Cf. AAS 87 (1995) 921–982, especially number 96.
45. Cf. HThK Vat. II, vol. 2, pp. 420–428 and Peter Hünermann, 'Gesucht: ein neues Paradigma des Petrusdienstes' in H. Schütte (ed.), *Im Dienst der einen Kirche: ökumenische Überlegungen zur Reform des Papstamtes*, Paderborn/ Frankfurt/ Main, 2000, pp. 189–218.
46. Cf. Grimm, *ibid.*, footnote 39.
47. *Ibid.*, p. 637.
48. Cf. Peter Hünermann, 'Dogmatik 1949–1997. Wandlungen einer Disziplin' in Gerhard Fürst (ed.), *Zäsur: Generationswechsel in der katholischen Theologie*, Stuttgart, 1997, pp. 9–27.; Margit Eckholt, *Poetik der Kultur*, Freiburg/ Basel/ Vienna, 2002.
49. Cf. Reiner Kacynski, 'Angriff auf die Liturgiekonstitution? Anmerkung zu einer neuen Übersetzer-Instruktion' *Stimmen der Zeit* 126 (2001), pp. 651–668. HThk Vat. II, vol. 2, pp. 110f.

IV. A Panel on Vatican II Tomorrow

Vatican II Today

JOSEPH DORÉ

It would have very difficult for me to refuse the friendly suggestion made by Alberto Melloni that I should contribute to the final section of this special volume of *Concilium* designed to mark the fortieth anniversary of Vatican II. I do in effect feel a very strong relationship with that great church event, for at least three reasons.

1. Ordained priest at the end of 1961, and so before the opening of the Council, I had the great luck to do part of my studies in Rome just when it was in progress. I can still see myself, a young student lodging at the Saint-Sulpice *Procure*, brought into contact with a number of bishops and theologians, but above all sharing in their 'joys and hopes, . . . griefs and . . . anxieties', to adopt the vocabulary that would become that of the monument to the Council, its constitution *Gaudium et Spes*. I have never forgotten those times. And I might be allowed to add that a short while later, reading that newcomer among theological reviews that bore the suggestive name of *Concilium* was not without importance in my theological thinking, in full development at that time.

2. Having become a theologian, I was led to specialize in Christology, ecclesiology, and apologetics, then in theology of religions. In all these fields, the Council documents became a major source for me from the moment they were published, to the point that I could recite entire chunks of documents such as *Lumen Gentium* and *Dei Verbum* by heart – and in Latin as well as in French! When I became a teacher at the major seminary in Nantes, then director of the Carmelite seminary in Paris while also teaching at the neighbouring faculty of theology, one part of my work consisted in commenting on the council documents, comparing them with tradition and experience,

making the students love them, checking the degree to which they were being applied.

3. Now, as a bishop, I do in practice carry out my responsibilities in line with the basic insights of the Council. I have experienced my episcopal ordination as entering into the fullness of the sacrament of Orders but also as joining a college called to bear mutual responsibility for the Church, in communion with the successor of Peter. Sometimes I think of the bishops of my young days and of my time in the seminary, for whom the episcopate was to be experienced as a 'dignity' with a still uncertain sacramental frame of reference and as a 'subalternate' responsibility in a very highly centralized church. I have to say that I am happy to be a bishop in the mould of the Second Vatican Council.

In the light of that triple experience, my contribution here will be a sort of situated and thought out 'defence and illustration' of that great council. I am truly, in all that I do, a determined partisan as a Christian, as a theologian, and as a pastor, at a time when some people, we are told, would like to call the whole Council more or less basically into question once more....

I shall divide my contribution into three sections. First, I propose to show that, after the Council, nothing will ever be quite the same as before. I shall then examine which aspects of the Council seem to me to have been best received, as well as what seems, on the other hand, still to require an effort from the Church. Finally, I shall sketch the courses of action that I feel should be devised to enable the great adventure embarked on forty years ago to bear fruit for us today.

I. Nothing will ever be quite the same as before

'Nothing will ever be quite the same as before': this was the title under which the review *Esprit et Vie* published the address I gave to a colloquy held from 11 to 14 March 1999 at the château of Klingenthal in Alsace, devoted to the final session of Vatican II.[1]

It seems appropriate to re-visit here, as my first sub-title, something that is not a slogan but a genuine manner of expressing an effective summary of this council, which defined *a before and an after* in the life of the Catholic Church in such a clear way that a great many ecclesial events can in effect be clearly placed in relation to it.

My attention was drawn by a very recent lecture that Mgr Piero Marini, Master of pontifical liturgical celebrations, gave in Naples in November 2003, published in French in *La Documentation Catholique* shortly afterwards.[2] Pontifical liturgy, with which this text is concerned, is hardly a domain in which one would expect to find very significant changes. And yet this is what its master has to say on the subject:

> To understand the change [. . .] we need take only one example: the Sovereign Pontiff's entrance into celebrations. Until the council, the pope, on the occasion of great solemnities, entered St Peter's basilica to the sound of silver trumpets, wearing the tiara, gloves, slippers in the liturgical colour; he was carried on 'manback' by the group of chair-bearers, flanked by *flabelli* (fan-carriers) and by a cloud of disparate personages, lay people and prelates, each wearing the uniform of his function, and who represented the nobility, the Roman patriarchy, the various bodies of guards, and other dignitaries of the papal court. It was planned as a solemn entrance, which gave the impression of the pope as a prince of this world surrounded by his court.
>
> Since the council, we have become used to seeing the pope taking part in an entrance procession into the Vatican basilica, dressed as a bishop of the Catholic Church [. . .], surrounded not by dignitaries of the papal court but by the concelebrants and ministers who have a part to play in the celebration.³

Reading this account shows us comprehensively why we can say that after the Council 'nothing will ever be quite the same as before': there are things that seemed normal and usual fifty years ago and which have become virtually intolerable today. Between then and now – a relatively short span of time – an event took place that made what most of the faithful previously accepted without a problem appear outmoded and obsolete: that event was, obviously, the Second Vatican Council.

It might be objected that in starting with the liturgy I have chosen an easy field, so obvious is it that this area – which clearly involves so much that appeals to the senses of sight and sound – has witnessed the most spectacular changes. The example provided by Mgr Marini is nevertheless one that can show us that the main changes that have come about are not in the outer order, even if the externals are very striking. These are actually some of the *inner* changes that have effectively been made:

— On what might be called the anthropological level, the refusal to see a man, whatever his dignity and the eminence of his office, carried by other men and surrounded by exaggerated signs of honour;
— On the ecclesiological level, the renunciation by the church of earthly power and its attributes, which correlates to the rediscovery of the pope's original function, that of being Bishop of Rome;

– On the theological level, the quest for a greater conformity with Christ, who did not enter Jerusalem in great splendour but as one sent by the Lord who comes to serve and not to be served.

In my 1999 lecture I stressed above all the deep *ecclesiological* changes for which we have Vatican II to thank. Following a distinction dear to that council, which has been criticized as artificial but from which there is nevertheless no turning back, I distinguished two levels to this ecclesiological change: that of the *internal* organization and workings of the church and the *external* one of mutual understanding between the church and the world. I refer readers to the text for how I developed this thesis. Here I shall just go a little deeper into the liturgical example I have just begun to analyze.

(a) The internal organization and workings of the church.

Here a first change concerns the basic conception the Church had of itself. The triumphal *cortège* that took place before the liturgical reform initiated by the Council corresponded to a 'vision of the church that described and conceived it above all as a hierarchical society constituted and functioning on the basis of its single summit, both in the order of government and in that of teaching and actions.'[4]

The move from the showy *cortège* to the liturgical procession means, then, much more a desire for a return to simplicity. It expresses theologically the move away from a juridical-administrative conception of the Church (one in which the distribution of power counts for most) to the adoption of a historical-salvific approach. It calls for the conversion of a Church-power to a Church-communion.

The second ecclesiological change, which is also a decisive one, comes from the fact that the pope has renounced the greater part of those external trappings that set him aside so clearly from the other bishops. This point refers us back to the great decisions the Council made on bishops: proclaiming their sacramentality, recognizing their collegiality, but also developing Episcopal Conferences and creating a Synod of Bishops, all combining to call for and put into effect the 'effective organization of a type of episcopal collaboration that had nor previously existed'[5] – in recent centuries, at least.

(b) Understanding of the reciprocal relationship between church and world

We can clearly see the course followed from, on one side, a Church anxious to affirm its authority over nations and their leaders, a church in which its head defined himself as – and appeared to be – a temporal sovereign, and, on the other, the Church of today. We have moved form a model of 'Christendom', that of a church that declared itself a 'perfect society', sovereign in relation to and other civil or political power. Now, with Vatican II, we have discovered a church that recognizes, along with the rightful autonomy of political power, the right to religious freedom.

Who today could tolerate a church that claimed to take the place of temporal powers, a pope who tended to behave like a political sovereign in struggles (even armed struggles) against others. This view has become just as unbearable outside the church, for those who denounce nostalgic temptations to clerical power, as it has for Christians themselves – or at least for the majority of them. . . . It really is quite true that, after Vatican II, 'nothing will ever be quite the same as before', as much for the Church in itself as for its proper relationship with the world in which it is called to live.

II. Theological and pastoral: a reversed relationship

As we know, Vatican II defined itself above all as a 'pastoral' council. Its proceedings, its 'style' – as I called it in the lecture cited above – aimed at being different from those of most of the councils that preceded it over two thousand years of the Church's history. Indeed, the purpose assigned to it at the outset by Pope John XXIII was not to work out a set of dogmatic expressions that would then be translated into new statement (graded by obligation of adherence to them) while at the same time condemning erroneous and dangerous doctrines (of which several were nevertheless pointed out as such).

Having said that, we need at once to add a corollary, in view of the way in which some adversaries of the Council have tried to use the style it sought to adopt as means of relativizing the importance of the documents it produced, by calling them '*only* pastoral document'. Let us make no mistake: Vatican II clearly, fairly and squarely, carried out a *theological* task – more so, undoubtedly, than many previous councils together.

In this respect, it is worth stressing first the decisive position occupied by theologian 'experts' – *periti* – at all stages of the Council's progress, starting with the pre-preparatory phase, in which a large number of bishops judiciously appealed to theologians for help in drafting the contribution they has been asked for – at first, that is, an itemised list of the subjects they would like to see tackled by the Council. It is equally worth underlining the fact that the theologians' contribution did not lessen as the Council progressed: it was made in the open as well as in the corridors, and particularly through the many afternoon conferences organized in Rome by the bishops of various language groups. Finally, we should not ignore the numerous and varied theological contributions that, at the end of the Council, enabled its great intuitions to be translated into guidelines and decrees to be applied.

Was it then 'a council of experts', as some have claimed? The phrase is not an accurate assessment, as the bishops never ceased to have their hands on the tiller. It is, though, quite legitimate to speak of a council closely linked to the evolution of theology, in a relationship that was also reciprocal. Vatican II would not have been what it was if it had not been preceded by a lively 'theological movement', just as this movement would not have borne some of its finest fruits without the powerful springboard the Council proved to be for the theologians.

Moving on now from the preparation and course of the Council to the question of the acceptance it commanded, I should like to propose this thesis, which I shall go on to justify: the reception of the Council called 'more pastoral than theological' has in fact been greater and better in the theological circles than in the world of pastoral realities!

(a) The reception of Vatican II in theological circles

This council, conceived and experienced theologically, could *a priori* only be well received in theological circles. And in fact there has been no break between theological research as such and the texts the Council produced: did they not reflect that very theological research in themselves? At last some of them, furthermore, fairly and squarely marked a stage in a dynamic process almost naturally destined to be pursued.

Studies of episcopal collegiality have not ceased since the day *Lumen gentium* was promulgated. It was indeed itself an invitation to undertake them. Also, the Council did not claim to be expressing the final word on the subjects it treated, only to be pointing out the direction in which further reflection should develop.

The theology of the laity obeyed the same principle: we can see that it has been considerably developed today, including in the area of ministeriality, which the Council itself hardly tackled, limiting itself rather the presence of lay people in the world. Today, however, we are able to see more clearly that a sensible theology of the laity cannot be conceived in practice without linking the indispensable presence of lay people in secular situations with their *suitable* involvement in properly ministerial tasks.

In the end there is no denying that ecumenism and inter-religious dialogue have, in general, made considerable progress in theology.[6] In this area, the signature of the joint Lutheran-Catholic declaration on justification is a 'sign of the times' of the greatest significance.[7]

Here we have to realize that 'receiving' the Council is in no way being content just to note its achievements, as the ambiguous expression 'nothing but the Council' could lead people to believe. 'Receiving' the Council means digging the furrow it began to mark out. Theologians are working on this.

(b) The reception of Vatican II in pastoral situations

Correlatively, in the pastoral field, it would seem that we can note both significant advances and very disappointing hesitations.

– Among the major advances, I would cite the installation of a renewed permanent deaconate within the overall ministerial structure of the Church. On this aspect I am delighted to be able to point out that, and how, the Catholic ministerial structure is now the richest and most diversified of any of the Christian confessions. From now on, it embraces three very degrees of ministry – with the states of life required of each – at the heart of the same sacrament of Orders, with, in addition, the field left open to lay ministries.

I also note, in the pastoral field itself, the spectacular progress of ecumenical and interreligious dialogue, made possible by recognition of the principle of religious freedom, amongst other factors. How could the Assisi meeting have taken place if the council had not passed that way earlier? And what can one say of the fine fruits of dialogue and prayer in common not only with our separated Protestant and Orthodox brethren, but also with our Jewish 'elder brothers' and Muslim friends?

– Yet there are also hesitations. I see them above in relation to the great theological advances made in the Constitution *Lumen gentium*. On the one hand they concern the nature of the relationship between the college of bishops and the pope, and on the other – still more fundamental – the nature of the church itself as people of God. Have we really drawn out the full consequences of the affirmation of the church as being in the first place the assembly of all those who would believe in Christ, before enquiring into the distinctions of order and degree to be observes among them? *Lumen gentium* nevertheless presented the mystery of the Church in global fashion before, from n.18 onward, examining its hierarchical structure.

The call of the whole Church to holiness, dealt within Chapter V, has no doubt been greatly honoured through the numerous beatifications and canonizations carried out by John Paul II, who had been a council father, but is it really taken seriously in our catechesis?

Even if great step forward have been taken, we have still to draw the conclusions from a certain number of principles laid down or recalled in the area of *liturgy*. Here, the hesitations have sometimes looked more like steps backward. While the reform was largely designed to give access to the paschal mystery, to its celebration, weekly through the Sunday Eucharist, annually on the occasion of the Easter *Triduum*, many places are seeing a resurfacing of devotions that risk obscuring the meaning of this. Was it really necessary to introduce the feasts of St Rita or of Padre Pio into the *universal* calendar? And what happened, in many places, to implementing the great desire to cut down on saints' days to give more emphasis to the Sunday celebration?

III. The last of the councils?

An intervention by Cardinal Martini at one of the last synods was interpreted by the press as a call to summon a Third Vatican Council: he then had to clarify his remarks, explaining that in truth what he was expressing a wish for was a continuation of the conciliar process rather than the calling of a new council as such.

I have to say that I am happy with such a view of the question.

In a certain sense, Vatican II marked a limit: 2,500 bishops from all over the world gathered in St Peter's basilica, called upon to pronounce on most of the issues associated with Christian life, in the course of sessions spread over three years! Today, the number of Catholic bishops has almost doubled, and, more importantly, the cultural origins are far more diverse. While Africa and Asia were had a presence at Vatican II, they were in many cases represented by *missionary* bishops originating from Europe or North America. All the bishops were furthermore asked to speak in Latin, in many had done a good part of their theological studies, and only some Eastern bishops refused to bow to this rule. How would it be possible today to ensure adequate communication among all the participants of a hypothetical Vatican III?

The physical conditions would certainly pose a serious problem to such a gathering, but one could still add that such a doubly universal council – through the number of participants and of the subjects they would tackle – does not necessarily seem desirable. Bishops need to exchange views among themselves; such an assembly, one might well fear, would be so solemn and formal in character that any meaningful exchange would undoubtedly be seriously compromised.

(a) A local conciliar process

The experience of Bishops' Conferences shows both the necessity for and the benefits of regular meetings among bishops from the same geographical region. Why, then, could 'provincial councils' – there is no need to hesitate in using this designation, as Canon Law itself does so fairly and squarely – not be held at local level, at national level, and perhaps at continental level?

Such assemblies could base themselves on an irrefutable historical church tradition, from Christian antiquity to recent times. Would there not be several reasons for the bishops of Black Africa, to take just them as an example, to be able (in effective communion with Rome, of course) to gather together in the form of a council, in order to deal with the specific to their continent – liturgical inculturation, local marriage customs, tribal problems . . .? The same question could also, *mutatis mutandis* of course and also only by way of example, be applied to the bishops of France. Their Bishops' Conference does indeed meet at regular intervals, but the terms and conditions of these annual or biennial gatherings do not exhaust the possibilities one can envisage for collaboration among them.

(b) An international conciliar process

While Vatican II defined itself indistinctly as 'this most sacred Council' (as at the beginning of the Constitution on the Liturgy) or 'this most sacred Synod' (in the first sentence of Dei Verbum), we have got into the habit of using 'Synod of Bishops' to designate the regular gatherings of delegates from the national episcopates around the pope to deal with such and such a subject in need of discussion. This institution of the synod is a fruit of the Council. Announced by Pope Paul VI on 14 September 1965 in his opening address to the fourth session, it effectively allows the bishops of the entire world to express themselves regularly, through those they have delegated. The participants in these assemblies also reflect the cultural catholicity of the church, since they come from all continents.

We have to admit however that at least up till no, this exercise only partially realizes the ideal of *conciliarity* that could be developed at all levels in the Church. For one thing, since the subjects for discussion have been fairly strictly defined in advance, it is hardly possible for the assembled bishops to modify the order of the day substantially and so make their particular current priorities feature. For another, the outcome of each synodal session is presented in the form of a post-synodal Exhortation, which, even it is an accurate reflection of the tone of the debates, is still a clear pulling-back from a council in which all the documents have been approved through the votes of a majority of the bishops themselves. While remaining, obviously, in communion with the Bishop of Rome, could the synod itself not find a better ay of expressing its own convictions and its own views?

(c) An irreversible process

As I have said already: the Second Vatican Council made an impression originally through the new 'style' it brought. Having said this, one has to add that, recognized as it was by Catholics as the twenty-first ecumenical council, it will perhaps prove to have been the last of a model that it has perhaps brought at once to its apogee and its full term.

On the other hand, Vatican II will have sown the seeds of *synodality* or *conciliarity* at every level of the church. There will be no more parishes, and certainly no more dioceses, without their pastoral councils. . . . And every nation will have its bishops' Conference. . . . The 'monarchical' figure, essential to Catholic ecclesiology (one parish priest per parish, one bishop per diocese, one pope in the universal church), has certainly not been denied; it has, however, been fortunately completed and balanced by this synodality, which brings a real enrichment on all levels. On the one hand, each officer in the hierarchy is now accompanied by a *council*, while on the other those responsible on the same level find themselves called to meet regularly together for a *collegial* exercise of their responsibility.

It would seem that this process, already well advanced, is irreversible. Vatican II will thus have contributed to the movement from *a church that summons councils* to *a church that lives conciliarly*. Is this not, in the end, the finest inheritance that this council could have left to us, and is the best homage we can pay to it not to recognize this progress and to allow it to continue?

Translated by Paul Burns

Notes

1. J. Doré, 'Rien ne sera plus tout à fait comme avant', *Esprit et Vie* 19 (Oct. 2000), pp. 3–11.
2. P. Marini, 'Liturgé et beauté: experiences de renouveau de certaines celebrations pontificales', *La Documentation Catholique* 2323 (7 Nov. 2004), pp. 909–18. The original Italian text appeared in the review *Asprenas* 50 (2003).
3. Marini, *art. cit.*, p. 910.

4. Doré, *at. cit.*, p. 5.
5. *Ibid.*, p. 7.
6. See J. Doré, 'Aspects de la reception de *Nostra Aetate* ans l'Église de France', *La Documentation Catholique* 2227 (4 June 2000), pp. 525–31.
7. J. Doré, 'Enjeux et contenu de la Déclaration commune luthéro-catholique sur la justification', *Documents-Épiscopat* 14 (Oct. 1999), 8pp.
8. See J. Doré and M. Vidal (eds), *Des ministres pour l'Église*, Paris 2002.

Humanity – Centre and Summit of the Earth

LUKAS VISCHER

At the end of the Third Session of the Council (1964) the Decree on Ecumenism was passed. This marked a kind of turning point. The Roman Catholic Church which previously been extremely reticent about contacts with other Churches now made a commitment before the whole world to co-operate actively in the 'restoration of unity'. She declared explicitly her willingness to participate in the Ecumenical Movement which was already under way in other Churches. This step, as would soon be apparent, was to have the effect of a breach in the dyke. Within a very short time the walls which had only recently been so carefully guarded began to fall. Christians of all denominations began to regard each other as brothers and sisters. The 21 November 1964 will therefore remain a memorable date in the annals of the Ecumenical Movement.

Instantly the question arose what the concrete consequences of the Decree would be. The Council was not yet over. The issues on the agenda of the Fourth Session were something like a test case. There should be a debate about the 'mission of the Church'. Would be achievable to formulate a common understanding of the mission of the Church or at least to lay the foundations for a joint formulation and praxis? Above all the Council should deal with the witness of the 'Church in the modern world'. Since the end of the First Session it had been clear that the Council should not merely be concerned with the Church's internal problems, but that it should dare set out its place in the modern world. A Council not merely *ad intra* but also *ad extra*. Again and again it was said that the Council had ultimately come together to 'read the signs of the times'. What would the effect of the Decree on Ecumenism on this experiment be? Would it be possible 'to read the signs of the times *together*' or at least to lay the foundation for reading them together in the future?

Between the Third and Fourth Session there was an intensive interchange about these questions. The hopes were only partially fulfilled. Both the Decree on Ecumenism and the Pastoral Constitution on the 'Church in the Modern World' speak explicitly about the necessity to find agreement with the 'separated brethren'. Yet a actual joint reading was not achieved. The Pastoral Constitution remained a word from the *Roman Catholic Church* to the world. And up to the present day the Roman Catholic Church works on the assumption that she alone is responsible for the witness of *the Church* in the world.

On 8 December 1965 there was a big manifestation on St Peter's Square to mark the end of the Council. A number of speakers addressed in the name of the Church different sectors of the public – scientists, workers etc. – and offered them on the basis of the Pastoral Constitution an open and transparent dialogue.

What does this mean forty years later? Was the Pastoral Constitution really the world of the Church which had to be heard? Reading this text once again today, it is not merely doubt that arises in my mind with regard to this question. More and more I come to the conclusion that the Council itself has enacted an option which does not do justice to the 'signs of the times'. The Pastoral Constitution was no prophetic word. With this text the Church primarily accommodated the spirit of the 1960s.

The Constitution certainly had a considerable effect. It made an essential contribution to the changing public image of the Roman Catholic Church. It added new weight to the social engagement of the Church. Shortly after the Council Pope Paul VI went deeper with regard to the initial starting points of the Council in his encyclical *Populorum progressio*. What is remarkable from a contemporary point of view is the fact that there is no reference to the ecological crisis. The subject of the text are human beings who thanks to their intelligence and their extraordinary gifts are able to dominate nature more and more. They are called to build a more just and humane society. Surely the text also mentions the ambiguity of human action, but its emphasis is on the scientific and moral achievements of which human beings are capable. No mention of the destructions which human beings have brought about in God's creation, of the plundering of resources and the pollution of water, air and soil.

It would not be fair to the authors of the Constitution to accuse them of this deficiency. At the time of the Council only few were able to see the enormity of the ecological crisis. Although the discoveries in the area of atomic research had woken up some, confidence in science and technology was yet unbroken. Ongoing economic growth did not seem to throw up any problems but could be praised without restrictions. The priority of the Council was to make contact with the modern world. It is therefore understandable that it did not enter into a critical analysis of the modern world. During the following years, mainly since 1990, the magisterium has emphasized different points. The threat that human beings will call into question their own survival on this planet is mentioned in several papal texts and there are not only a few calls to more responsibility with regard to the gifts of creation. Can we therefore say that the deficiencies of the Constitution have in the meantime be corrected and resolved?

In my opinion the problem of the Pastoral Constitution is a more profound one. The ecological crisis raises the question about the place of the whole of humanity in creation. Who are we, human beings, amidst all of God's creatures? What role do we have? There are many who accuse the Jewish-Christian tradition of having contributed to today's ecological destruction. Several arguments are brought forward. First of all reference is made to the commission which God gave human beings when he created them: 'Be fruitful and multiply, and fill the earth and subdue it; and have dominion over the fish of the sea and over the birds of the air and over every living thing that moves upon the earth.' (Gen. 1.28) The critics add that the emphasis on God being totally Other in the Christian tradition calls into question the divine character of nature and thus cuts the ground from under the reverence for life. The Christian faith degrades nature top being a mere object and thus put into the hands of humans.

It is easy to show that this accusation is based on a misinterpretation of the biblical texts. The vocation of human beings is not to rule the world but to care for it. The testimony of the Old Testament in its entirety is a call to gratitude towards the creator. Several psalms are dedicated to this topic. Israel lives in contact with the earth. It was convinced that it had received Canaan from God himself as its dwelling place. It was conscious of the responsibility that came with this gift. It had to take care that the land remained fertile. A long list of Old Testament laws refers to this responsibility. We can think of the laws referring to sowing and harvest. We can think of the sabbath law, the obligation to refrain from work on the seventh day and to let the earth rest. Ecological imperatives are central to the Torah, the Jewish law, in contrast to the Roman law. The thesis that human beings are called to rule over nature is not a biblical perspective. It is nothing but the creed of humanity in modernity.

Now we must add immediately that the Christian tradition, and the Churches of the West in particular did not always hold this biblical view in high regard. Since Augustine an unbiblical anthropocentrism has come to the fore in Christian theology. There has been an overemphasis on the special role of human beings in creation. They are the aim and the crown of creation. They are the image of God and they alone have the ability to respond to God's call. The gift of reason raises them above all other creatures, and thus they are the measure of all things. The fact that they are, according to the testimony of the Bible, part of creation is pushed into the background. There can be hardly any doubt that such an understanding of humanity has contributed to the ecological unreason particularly of the nations of the West and continues to do so up to the present day.

And it is precisely here that we find the weakness of the Pastoral Constitution. In a manner almost reminiscent of caricature it joins into this overemphasis. It asks: what does the Church think about humanity? Which orientations does she need to suggest with regard to building society today? What is ultimately the significance of humanity in the universe? Her response then opens with the succinct sentence: 'According to the almost unanimous opinion of believers and unbelievers alike, all things on earth should be related to man as their center and crown.' (GS 12). Thus the tone for the rest of the response is set. Let us listen to what the text has to say about human beings:

> Man judges rightly that by his intellect he surpasses the material universe, for he shares in the light of the divine mind. By relentlessly employing his talents through the ages he has indeed made progress in the practical sciences and in technology and the liberal arts. In our times he has won superlative victories, especially in his probing of the material world and in subjecting it to himself. Still he has always searched for more penetrating truths, and finds them. For his intelligence is not confined to observable data alone, but can with genuine certitude attain to reality itself as knowable, though in consequence of sin that certitude is partly obscured and weakened. (GS 15)

Or: Only in freedom can man direct himself toward goodness. Our contemporaries make much of this freedom and pursue it eagerly; and rightly to be sure.... Man achieves such dignity when, emancipating himself from all captivity to passion, he pursues his goal in a spontaneous choice of what is good, and procures for himself through effective and skilful action, apt helps to that end. Since man's freedom has been damaged by sin, only by the aid of God's grace can he bring such a relationship with God into full flower.

Do such extracts not make clear that the Constitution has not only not recognized the ecological crisis but has even made emphases which point in the opposite direction? *With its theses about the role of human beings in the whole of creation it has basically made the creed of modernity its own.*

Let us once more go back to the beginning. Looking back to the Council forty years later shows how much many of its statements are stuck in the experience of the 1960s. This applies to what it says about the Ecumenical Movement. The Decree on Ecumenism has triggered a number of developments. A new situation has emerged. Together we have to analyze and interpret it. A new beginning is called for. This also applies to the Council's attempts to read the signs of the times. The Constitution on the Church in the modern world proves totally insufficient for today. The horizons have shifted in many ways over the past four decades. We are facing new challenges which are calling for a response. Signs of the times which have hitherto remained unheeded have become unmistakably visible. Should we therefore not find ways to read them and to respond to them *together*?

Translated by Natalie K. Watson

Contributors

GIUSEPPE ALBERIGO was born in Cuasso al Monte in the Italian province of Varese in 1926. He is professor of history at the Political Sciences faculty of the University of Bologna and secretary of the Institute for Religious Sciences in Bologna. He also edits the four-monthly review *Cristianesimo nella Storia*, is a member of the Committee of Honour of the *Revue des Sciences Religieuses*, and a corresponding member of *The Catholic Historical Review*. He is a doctor *honoris causa* from faculties in Germany and France. He is editor-in-chief of the five-volume *History of the Second Vatican Council*, published in six languages. His other publications include *Chiesa concilare. Identità e significato del conciliarismo* (1981), *La chiesa nella storia* (1988), *Il cristianesimo in Italia* (1989), *Papa Giovanni 1881–1963* (2000).

Address: Via G. Mazzini 82, I-40138 Bologna, Italy

ERIK BORGMAN, born in 1957 in Amsterdam, is married, father of two daughters and a lay dominican. From 1976 to 1984 he studied Theology and Philosophy at the Catholic University of Nijmegen where in 1990 he was awarded a doctorate for a thesis on the significance of different forms of liberation theology for academic theology, published as *Sporen van de bevrijdende God* (1990). From 1989 to 2003 he worked for the Dutch domincans on a study of the historic background and present-day significance of the theology of Edward Schillebeeckx, published as *Edward Schillebeeckx: een theoloog in zijn geschiedenis*. Deel I: *Een katholieke cultuurtheologie (1914–1965)* (1999 (English translation: *Edward Schillebeeckx: a Theologian in his History. Part I: A Catholic Theology of Culture (1914–1965)* (2003)). Since 2004 he has been director of the Heyerdaal Institute of the Catholic University of Nijmegen, an interdisciplinary centre for theology, science and culture. He currently researches the meaning of the cultural and social significance of religion and the Christian faith and theology and the religious and theological significance of contemporary culture. He has published numerous scholarly and popular articles and two collection of essays

Alexamenos aanbidt zijn God (Alexamenos worships his God, 1994) and *Dominicaanse spiritualiteit: Een verkenning (Leuven/Berg en Dal: Tijdschrift voor Geestelijk Leven* (2000; English: *Dominican Spirituality: An Exploration*, 2002). He is editor of the *Tijdschrift voor Theologie* and a member of the Foundation Board of *Concilium*.

Address: Heyendaal Instituut, Erasmusplein 1, 6525 HT Nijmegen, The Netherlands
E-mail: E.Borgman@hin.ru.nl; Borgman-VanLeusden@hetnet.nl

JOSÉ COMBLIN was born in Brussels in 1923 and ordained priest in 1947. He gained a Doctorate of Theology from the university of Louvain in 1950 and in 1958 moved to Latin America, first to Campinas (São Paulo, Brazil). He lectured at the theology faculty of the Catholic University of Santiago de Chile from 1962 to 1965, when he returned to Brazil, to the Theology Institute of Recife, where he stayed till 1972. He then moved back to Chile, to Talca, from 1972 to 1980, returning to João Pessoa in Brazil to take charge of lay missionary leadership training till 2005. He is the author of *The Holy Spirit and Liberation* (1989) and his latest works are *O caminho, Paulus* (*Paul, the Way*, 2004) and *O que é a verdade?* (*What is Truth?* 2005.).

Address: Cx.P. 13 Bayeux, 58.306-970 PB, Brazil
E-mail: monicamuggler@terra.com.br

PETER HÜNERMANN was born in Berlin in 1929 and studied philosophy and theology in Rome. He gained his doctorate in 1958 and his Habilitation in 1967 in Freiburg im Breisgau. From 1971 to 1982 he was professor of dogmatics in Munich and from 1973 to 2002 president of the Stipendienwerk Lateinamerika-Deutschland which he founded in 1968 with Bernhard Welte. From 1989 to 1995 he was founder president and from 1995 honorary president of the European Society for Catholic Theology and from 1996 to 2002 founder president of the International Network of Societies of Catholic Theology. His most recent book is *Dogmatische Prinzipienlehre. Glaube – Überlieferung – Theologie als Sprache und Wahrheitsgeschehen* (Münster 2003).

Address: Engwiesenstrasse 14, 72108 Rottenburg, Germany
E-mail: peter.huenermann@uni-tuebingen.de

HANS KÜNG, born 1928 in Sursee (Switzerland). 1948–1957 philosophical and theological studies at the Gregorian University, the Sorbonne and the Institut Catholique de Paris. 1962–1965 official theological consultant (Peritus) to the Second Vatican Council appointed by Pope John XXIII. 1960–1963 Professor of Fundamental Theology, 1963–80 Professor of Dogmatic and Ecumenical Theology at the Faculty of Catholic Theology and Director of the Institute for Ecumenical Research at the University of Tübingen; since 1980 Professor of Ecumenical Theology and Director of the Institute for Ecumenical Research at the University of Tübingen. 1996 Professor emeritus and President of the Fundation for a Global Ethic (Weltethos). Honorary Degrees from several universities.

Küng is coeditor of several journals and has written many books, including *Justification*, *The Council and Reunion*, *The Church*, *Infallible?*, *On Being a Christian*, *Does God Exist?*, *Eternal Life?*, *Christianity and the World Religions*, *Theology for the Third Millennium*, *Christianity and the Chinese Religions*, *Reforming the Church Today*, *Global Responsibility*, *Judaism*, *Credo*, *Great Christian Thinkers*, *Christianity*, *A Dignified Dying* (together with Prof. Walter Jens), *Global Ethics for Global Politics and Economics* (1997), *The Catholic Church. A Short History* (2001), *Der Islam. Geschichte, Gegenwart, Zukunft* (2004). Co-editor: *A Global Ethic. The Declaration of the Parliament of the World's Religions*. Editor: *Yes to a Global Ethic*.

Address: Waldhäuserstrasse 23, D-72076 Tübingen, Germany.

HERVÉ LEGRAND was born in 1935 and is a Dominican. He holds a degree in philosophy, a diploma in canon law, and a doctorate in theology and has studied at the Saulchoir in Paris and the universities of Strasbourg, Thomas Aquinas (in Rome), and Athens. He is professor emeritus of the Paris theology faculty, where he directed the doctorate course of studies, and of the Higher Institute for Ecumenical Studies, as well as a former professor at the faculty of canon law. He has been a member of international commissions for dialogue between the Catholic Church and Pentecostals and the World Lutheran Federation, and he currently serves on French commissions for dialogue with the Orthodox Church and the with the Reformed Lutheran Church.

Address: 20 rue des Tanneries, Paris, France
email: hervelegrandop@yahoo.fr

ALBERTO MELLONI teaches contemporary history at the University of Modena and Reggio Emilia; he is a member of the XXIII Foundation for Religious Studies, Bologna, on the board of *Christianesimo nella storia* and a member of the board of directors of *Concilium*. He has written extensively on the history and institutions of Christianity from the Middle Ages (*Innocenzo IV*, preface by B. Tierney, Genoa 1990) to the twentieth century: he worked on John XXIII (*Tra Istanbul, Atene e la guera. A.G. Roncalli vicario e delegato apostolico 1935 – 1944*, Genoa 1993; *Il Giornale dell'Anima Giovanni XXIII*, Milan 2000), on Vatican II (as editor of the five volumes of *Storia del concilio Vaticano II diretta da G. Alberigo*, Bologna 1995 – 2001), on Vatican II diplomacy (*L' altra Roma. Politica e S. Sede durante il concilio Vaticano II, 1959 – 1965*, Bologna 2000), and on the conclave (*Il conclave. Storia di una instituzione*, Bologna 2001). His articles in different journals are devoted to the interplay between politics and religion.

Address: Via Crispi 6, 42100 Reggio Emilia, Italy
E-mail: albeto.melloni@tin.it

CHRISTOPH THEOBALD was born in Cologne in 1946 and became a Jesuit in 1978; he was ordained priest in 1982. He is professor of fundamental and dogmatic theology in the theology faculty of the Sèvres Centre in Paris. He is editor of *Recherches de Sciences Religieuse*, in which he writes regular reports on developments in systematic theology (specifically the doctrine of the Trinity). His publications include: *Maurice Blondel und das Problem der Modernität. Beitrag zu einer epistemologischen Standortbestimmung zeitgenössischer Fundamentaltheologie* (Frankfurt 1988); *La Révélation . . . tout simplement* (Paris 2001); *L'Esprit Créateur dans la pensée musicale de Jean-Sébastien Bach* (Brussels 2002); *Le cas Jésus-Christ* (Paris, 2002).

Address: 15, Rue Monsieur, F 75007 Paris

ANDRÉS TORRES QUEIRUGA was born in 1940 and holds doctorates in philosophy from the University of Santiago de Compostela and in theology from the Gregorian in Rome. He taught fundamental theology at the Theological Institute in Santiago from 1968 to 1987 and is currently professor of philosophy of religion at the university there. He is editor of *Encrucillada: Revista Galega de Pensamento Cristián*, as well as being on the editorial board of *Iglesia Viva*, an advisor to *Revista Portuguesa de Filosofia*, and a founding member of the Spanish Society for Sciences of Religion. His many published works include *La Revelación de Dios en la realización del hombre* (1977, trans. into Italian, Portuguese, and German), *Creo en Dios Padre* (5th ed. 1998), *El problema de Dios en la Modernidad* (1998), *Fin del cristianismo premoderno* (2000), *Repensar la resurrección* (2003), *Esperanza a pesar del mal* (2005).

Address: Facultade de Filosofía, Campus Sur, 1748 Santiago de Compostela, Spain
E-mail: atorres@usc.es

CONCILIUM

FOUNDERS

A. van den Boogaard
P. Brand
Y. Congar OP †
H. Küng
J.-B. Metz
K. Rahner SJ †
E. Schillebeeckx OP

FOUNDATION

Jan Peters SJ (President)
Paul Vos (Treasurer)
Erik Borgman
Alberto Melloni
Susan Ross
Felix Wilfred

DIRECTORS

Regina Ammicht-Quinn (Frankfurt, Germany)
Erik Borgman (Nijmegen, The Netherlands)
Christophe Boureux OP (Lyon, France)
Eamonn Conway (Limerick, Ireland)
Hille Haker (Frankfurt, Germany)
Diego Irarrazaval (Santiago, Chile)
Maureen Junker-Kenny (Dublin, Ireland)
Solange Lefevbre (Montreal, Canada)
Alberto Melloni (Reggio Emilia, Italy)
Eloi Messi Metogo (Yaoundé, Cameroun)
Susan Ross (Chicago, USA)
Janet Martin Soskice (Cambridge, UK)
Jon Sobrino SJ (San Salvador, El Salvador)
Luiz Carlos Susin (Porto Alegre, Brazil)
Andrés Torres Queiruga (Santiago de Compostela, Spain)
Marie-Theres Wacker (Münster, Germany)
Elaine Wainwright (Auckland, New Zealand)
Felix Wilfred (Madras, India)

General Secretariat: Erasmusplein 1, 6525 HT Nijmegen, The Netherlands
http://www.concilium.org
Manager: Baroness Christine van Wijnbergen

Concilium Subscription Information

February 2005/1: *Cyberspace – Cyberethics – Cybertheology*

April 2005/2: *Hunger, Bread and the Eucharist*

June 2005/3: *Christianity in Crisis?*

October 2005/4: *A Forgotten Future: Vatican II*

December 2005/5: *Islam: New Issues*

New subscribers: to receive *Concilium* 2005 (five issues) anywhere in the world, please copy this form, complete it in block capitals and send it with your payment to the address below.

Please enter my subscription for *Concilium* 2005

Individuals
____ £35.00 UK/Rest of World
____ $67.00 North America
____ €60.00

Institutions
____ £48.50 UK/Rest of World
____ $93.50 North America
____ €80.00.50

Please add £17.50/$33.50/€30 for airmail delivery

Payment Details:
Payment must accompany all orders and can be made by cheque or credit card
I enclose a cheque for £/$ _____ Payable to SCM-Canterbury Press Ltd
Please charge my Visa/MasterCard (Delete as appropriate) for £/$ _____
Credit card number _____
Expiry date _____
Signature of cardholder _____
Name on card _____
Telephone _____ E-mail _____

Send your order to *Concilium*, SCM-Canterbury Press Ltd
9–17 St Albans Place, London N1 0NX, UK
Tel +44 (0)20 7359 8033 Fax +44 (0)20 7359 0049
E-Mail: office@scm-canterburypress.co.uk

Customer service information:
All orders must be prepaid. Subscriptions are entered on an annual basis (i.e. January to December) No refunds on subscriptions will be made after the first issue of the Journal has been despatched. If you have any queries or require information about other payment methods, please contact our Customer services department.